Praise for *Inside the Minds*

"What C-Level executives read to keep their edge and make pivotal business decisions. Timeless classics for indispensable knowledge." - Richard Costello, Manager-Corporate Marketing Communication, General Electric (NYSE: GE)

"Want to know what the real leaders are thinking about now? It's in here." - Carl Ledbetter, SVP & CTO, Novell, Inc.

"Priceless wisdom from experts at applying technology in support of business objectives." - Frank Campagnoni, CTO, GE Global Exchange Services

"Unique insights into the way the experts think and the lessons they've learned from experience." - MT Rainey, Co-CEO, Young & Rubicam/Rainey Kelly Campbell Roalfe

"Unlike any other business book." - Bruce Keller, Partner, Debevoise & Plimpton

"The Inside the Minds series is a valuable probe into the thought, perspectives, and techniques of accomplished professionals. By taking a 50,000 foot view, the authors place their endeavors in a context rarely gleaned from text books or treatise." - Chuck Birenbaum, Partner, Thelen Reid & Priest

"A must read for anyone in the industry." - Dr. Chuck Lucier, Chief Growth Officer, Booz-Allen & Hamilton

"A must read for those who manage at the intersection of business and technology." - Frank Roney, General Manager, IBM

"A great way to see across the changing marketing landscape at a time of significant innovation." - David Kenny, Chairman & CEO, Digitas

"An incredible resource of information to help you develop outside-the-box..." - Rich Jernstedt, CEO, Golin/Harris International

"A snapshot of everything you need..." - Charles Koob, Co-Head of Litigation Department, Simpson Thacher & Bartlet

www.Aspatore.com

Aspatore Books is the largest and most exclusive publisher of C-Level executives (CEO, CFO, CTO, CMO, Partner) from the world's most respected companies. Aspatore annually publishes C-Level executives from over half the Global 500, top 250 professional services firms, law firms (MPs/Chairs), and other leading companies of all sizes. By focusing on publishing only C-Level executives, Aspatore provides professionals of all levels with proven business intelligence from industry insiders, rather than relying on the knowledge of unknown authors and analysts. Aspatore Books is committed to publishing a highly innovative line of business books, redefining and expanding the meaning of such books as indispensable resources for professionals of all levels. In addition to individual best-selling business titles, Aspatore Books publishes the following unique lines of business books: Inside the Minds, Business Bibles, Bigwig Briefs, C-Level Business Review (Quarterly), Book Binders, ExecRecs, and The C-Level Test, innovative resources for all professionals. Aspatore is a privately held company headquartered in Boston, Massachusetts, with employees around the world.

Inside the Minds

The critically acclaimed *Inside the Minds* series provides readers of all levels with proven business intelligence from C-Level executives (CEO, CFO, CTO, CMO, Partner) from the world's most respected companies. Each chapter is comparable to a white paper or essay and is a future-oriented look at where an industry/profession/topic is heading and the most important issues for future success. Each author has been carefully chosen through an exhaustive selection process by the *Inside the Minds* editorial board to write a chapter for this book. *Inside the Minds* was conceived in order to give readers actual insights into the leading minds of business executives worldwide. Because so few books or other publications are actually written by executives in industry, *Inside the Minds* presents an unprecedented look at various industries and professions never before available.

INSIDE THE MINDS

Inside the Minds:
The Business of Sports

C-LEVEL BUSINESS INTELLIGENCE · C-LEVEL BUSINESS INTELLIGENCE · C-LEVEL BUSINESS INTELLIGENCE

ASPATORE
BOOKS

Published by Aspatore, Inc.

For corrections, company/title updates, comments or any other inquiries please email info@aspatore.com.

First Printing, 2004
10 9 8 7 6 5 4 3 2 1

ISBN 1-58762-136-3 Library of Congress Control Number: 2004102495

Inside the Minds Managing Editor, Laura Kearns, Edited by Michaela Falls, Proofread by Eddie Fournier, Cover design by Scott Rattray & Ian Mazie

Inside the Minds:
The Business of Sports

Executives from Major Sports Franchises on How a Team Operates Behind the Scenes

CONTENTS

Winning On and Off the Field

Brian Cashman
Senior Vice President and General Manager
New York Yankees

Striking the Right Balance between Entertainment and Sports

In many aspects, sports is an entertainment business. The product being sold is the game and its wonderful unpredictability, presented by the manager's strategies and the players' abilities as entertainment to the paying public. And in the competitive sports arena, there is nothing more entertaining than winning.

From a business perspective, winning *on* the field typically results in profitability *off* the field. Winning affects an organization and its team in a multitude of ways, one of the most important being higher game attendance. Higher attendance increases fan revenues in the form of additional parking fees, more concession purchases, and a greater desire for team memorabilia. In turn, the increased profits from these outlets lead to improved merchandising and greater media exposure – all of which further enhances the team brand.

Winning also has an impact on much more than fan revenues. Profitable returns provide the financial latitude to attract, obtain, and equitably compensate the quality players and personnel who can extend a winning record. In short, winning begets more winning. And the team, the organization, and the fan base all benefit from games that have a positive outcome.

The Business Side of Sports

Being a sports manager differs very little from being a manager in any other industry. You look for dedicated people who share your goals and who are willing to make a serious time commitment -- day in and day out -- to attain those goals.

In sports the pressure to succeed is almost unrelenting, and a general manager (GM) seldom escapes scrutiny. As a GM you are graded on your success every day. A win equals pass; a loss equals fail. This is a very demanding way to work, and it does not suit everyone. It becomes especially difficult when one loss turns into several losses that then turn into a losing streak. Pressure comes to bear not only from the organization but also from the fans and the press. Conversely, there are times when you experience a number of great wins. Everyone, including the press, reacts positively and you feel a measure of both accomplishment and security.

There is no denying that the role of GM is a volatile, pressure-packed position. In order to manage the day-to-day demands effectively, it's important to surround yourself with people who are intelligent, calm, and efficient. You need to be able to rely on those who can objectively assess a situation, gather facts, dissect the problem, and find solutions.

Personally, when it comes to staffing I often look for people who hold an MBA or a law degree and who possess a keen intelligence. What is important is that we are all heading in the same direction and working toward the same goal – winning.

All Sports are Not Alike

Baseball differs from other sports in two major areas: the length of the season and the development of the players. The full season consists of spring training, a total of approximately 35 games, and the regular season schedule of 162 games played over 183 days with a 25-man roster. Because of the long season and the daily playing schedule, baseball players don't have an opportunity to rebound physically to the same extent as players in other sports. The conditioning of their muscles and their daily regimen must be adapted to address those demands.

Baseball also differs from other sports in that it requires a physical and mental honing of the players' craft over an extended period of time. You can enter the NFL right from college; you can enter the NBA right from high school or college. But high school or college players rarely move into major league baseball; in the entire history of the game, perhaps twenty players have been able to make this type of transition. Baseball has a high learning curve; as a result, becoming a major league player is a long process. Generally it takes four to six years of minor league professional experience before a baseball player will even be considered for the major leagues.

Baseball, in contrast to other sports, also relies on an extensive feeder system. The Yankees support six minor league franchises that include teams in the United States as well as a summer league in the Dominican Republic. Each of those teams requires a roster of about 23 players, a manager, a full coaching staff, trainers, and strength coaches. It is an expensive system to maintain. Injuries to your biggest assets, the players, are something that you better be prepared for in terms of prevention and rehabilitation programs.

The Role of a General Manager

The GM of a major league baseball team has a fundamental responsibility: build a winning team. As the senior vice president and general manager of the New York Yankees, I am charged with negotiating player contracts and constructing the major league club that we run every day. My role requires making the decisions that will lead us to our ultimate goal: winning a world championship.

To begin with, a GM needs to be a visionary. You must have the ability to envision the final product – a championship team. And you must have the skills – and the personnel in place – which will enable you to make that vision a reality. As a GM you must consider all of the fiscal constraints established by ownership as you're developing a team with the best chance of winning not only today but also tomorrow. My responsibilities include putting together a 25-man team that requires six coaches and a manager as well as a support staff that includes trainers, strength and conditioning coaches, psychologists, massage therapists, a hitting coach, a pitching coach, and outfield and infield instructors.

In many respects, a GM acts as a consensus builder among the various departments involved in managing a team, including player development, scouting, management, and coaching. A GM also directs the activities of a front office staff that offers support, administrative, and personnel functions. Each of the departments within a team organization has its own particular interests, and a GM must be cognizant of all of them.

While all of these various departments have the same collective interest - - developing a championship team -- individual interests may vary. It is the responsibility of the GM to ensure that everyone is working toward the same goal. Based on my experience, the most successful GMs are those who surround themselves with effective people who are empowered with resources, authority, and responsibility.

Running a Successful Major League Team

Effective team leadership does not depend solely on the players. The overall game strategy is also a vital determinant of how well a team's objectives are met. Operational strategies will vary depending on the organization's goals. A young franchise that is focused on developing a winning team will employ different strategies than those of a legendary team looking to extend its championship legacy.

As with any business entity, a baseball organization's plan or philosophy must be communicated and executed at every level. When determining how to execute your plan, you must consider the culture and structure of the ball club. The level of consistency and "buy in" you achieve regarding your plan will determine whether your efforts become magic or tragic.

The secret to success is surrounding yourself with individuals who support your goals, share your vision, and operate in a cohesive manner. Bringing all of these elements together can take years, especially if there are periods when the ball club is experiencing organizational and management changes. It's important that a GM assess the effectiveness of the organization at the end of every season and that you possess the flexibility to respond to changing dynamics.

Of course, securing exceptional player talent is always of paramount importance. Within every major league ball club you'll find the same basic structure for developing player talent: a minor league feeder system and an army of scouts on the amateur, professional, and international sides. Various teams may have different philosophies regarding the most efficient way to develop talent but, by and large, the process is conducted in a similar fashion.

There will be times when your belief in the championship caliber of your club is shaken by a losing streak. During such a streak, a GM typically will track individual player performance as well as review minor league results in an attempt to better the team through trades and acquisitions. There may be tremendous temptation, on the part of many within the organization, to question the ability and strategy of the team's manager. But a GM must remain confident, even under difficult circumstances, in his manager and coaches and in their expertise and choices.

The Yankees organization normally maintains a "win now" philosophy. During the mid to late 1980s we experienced a number of failed attempts to winning the American League Eastern Division. We changed our approach in the early 1990s and began a rebuilding mode in which our sole focus was the future. We were developing our system and putting the building blocks in place that would provide for a "win" mode in the future. Since 1995, we have been experiencing the positive results of sound decisions we made years ago; those decisions have resulted in a championship-caliber team.

At some point we will substitute our current "win now" philosophy for a "rebuilding" philosophy again if we want to sustain another long successful championship run.

Generating Excitement, Generating Revenues

Everything we do as a team, as an organization, is for the fans. The fan base, which is in actuality our customer base, is what supports us. In the world of sporting environments, being a major league baseball team in the Northeast is different from being a team anywhere else in the country. Fans in the Northeast -- Boston, New York, Philadelphia – live and die every day with their teams.

A passionate fan base allows us to generate revenue. The formula is simple: if you build a winner, they will come. For example, the Yankees have drawn 3 million fans to our stadium in the Bronx during each of the past five seasons. We have demonstrated that if you have a solid organization that fosters winning, the fans will come out and support you. And their support comes in various ways: buying tickets at the ballpark; watching games on cable television; and purchasing hats, shirts, jerseys, and other team memorabilia.

Fans are our greatest source of revenue; player payroll is our greatest expense. No other expense in our budget compares to that of salaries. In this age of skyrocketing salaries, player payroll is very, very costly. There are times when you draw up your player roster in the winter but what you actually end up putting into place during the season may be different. Any adjustments you might need to make in terms of players could impact your payroll and your bottom line.

The cost of doing business in baseball is significant. The Yankees support the major team, six minor league teams, an academy, and an army of personnel. Our support staff is also extensive and includes everyone from stadium operators and security staff to a ticket director and a marketing director to accounting personnel and legal experts.

During the past eight years, new approaches to revenue sharing in baseball have been developed. The commissioner's office ownership group ratified a new revenue agreement during 2003 in order to avoid a strike. As part of this new agreement, the terms of revenue sharing were increased dramatically. Because the Yankees are very successful, we are being called upon to assist other competitors within major league baseball. We are required by the new basic agreement to participate in a high degree of revenue sharing. We may also be required to pay luxury taxes based on our payroll.

From a business perspective, these changes require us, as an organization, to conduct ourselves more efficiently in regard to fiscal policies. A dollar earned is not a full dollar in our pockets any more; we might be making 75 cents or 50 cents on the dollar because we provide a portion of our profits to our competitors.

As a GM, it is not your job to *grow* revenues but you can *affec*t revenues by helping to develop a winning team. Having a winning team allows others in the organization to develop new ideas and concepts that capitalize on the team's success and generate new revenue streams. A successful team can bring about great advertising and marketing opportunities. A good example of this is the affiliation between Adidas and the Yankees. Our relationship with Adidas has developed a new revenue stream for the organization and world-wide exposure for Adidas. Everyone wants to be associated with a winner.

Growing the organization through international partnerships is another avenue for generating revenues. The Yankees have forged a relationship with the Yomiuri Giants of the Japanese Professional Baseball League; they are considered the Yankees of Japan. And we signed Japan's best player, Hideki Matsui, as a left fielder. These are ways in which an organization can extend its brand worldwide and create a larger fan base, which translates into a larger customer base.

Trading on the Future

A GM must not only assess the available talent, market conditions, and associated costs of current players; he or she must also provide reasonable projections regarding up-and-coming players available through the draft. You need to develop a system for comparing the value of veteran players and rookies with star potential.

In baseball a scouting director oversees drafts, which is a different process than what occurs in other sports. For instance, an NBA team will draft from need -- if they need a center, they will draft a center; if they lack a point guard, they will seek a point guard.

But because there are four to six years of nurturing players in the minor league system we focus on drafting an athlete who projects to be a terrific baseball player. You can't draft on need – you have to draft on the best available player whom you think will ultimately make it to the major leagues. We draft high-level players, but the outcome isn't always predictable. Many times the athletes considered most likely to succeed are the ones that don't make it. Then there are times when a "diamond in the rough" – the player who didn't make much money from a signing bonus – surprises you by honing his skills in such a way that he becomes the next MVP.

In building a championship club, the farm system is often used. As a feeder system, it allows you to develop the players that you will later put in place to have a championship-caliber club. We then use that system to trade for what we need at the big league level.

You can also use free agency to secure players for positions you need. But you can't build a club from free agency. You build your club through the farm system and through amateur and professional scouting; you finish off your club through free agency and trades.

Always having the best people in place to evaluate players is key. The scouting side identifies championship-caliber talent while the development side works to connect those players with the various programs that will get them to the major leagues. At times, the scouting and development departments disagree as to what is best for a player. The development side focuses on what is best for the player's future while managers and coaches are focused on winning today. Sometimes the desire to win now conflicts with what is best for the development of a player. Putting a player in a situation for which he is not fully prepared can result in a serious blow to his psyche, one he might not recover from.

The process of developing players is volatile and there are many hurdles along the way. I would compare it to the early life of a sea turtle which I learned from watching the Discovery Channel. When a sea turtle comes in from the ocean, it makes its way to the beach and lays a hundred eggs. When those hundred eggs hatch, all the little turtles make their way to the water but only about two will eventually survive to become adults. The life of a baseball prospect is similar in that way.

Assessing the Value of a Player

In the sports business, you have to look for talent, first and foremost. Scouts are expected to know the market value of players, which is essential in terms of negotiating a deal.

It's important to have people in place who are very skilled at evaluating players' physical abilities as well as their mental fortitude and character. Emotional and mental strength is essential if a player is to survive difficult times, slumps, and injuries.

Sometimes an organization may be looking at an international player; if you happen to be in a specific country where no one is aware of that particular player, then you have leverage. In that case, you can probably secure the player at a very reasonable price.

But if you are involved in a bidding war where a number of clubs are vying for the same player and the market value is the equivalent of a first-round pick, then securing that player may cost you close to a million dollars or more. At that point, you need to decide whether or not you want to negotiate at that level and assume the risks associated with that type of deal. Even players who have made it through the minor leagues may not achieve the performance level you expect to get for that amount of money.

You can try to limit your risk in regard to a player by securing disability insurance for injuries and life insurance on his contract. Both types of insurance are beneficial if the premiums are favorable. You cannot do that on every player because in today's markets securing insurance has become almost prohibitive.

Sometimes coaches are blamed unfairly for players' failures; sometimes the blame is warranted. Coaches are responsible for putting players in the best position to succeed and for guiding them through their slumps. There can be a lot of player turnover if someone is looking for a quick fix, but in our business there are no immediate answers. Ultimately, players are responsible for their successes or failures -- and they are being paid a large sum of money to succeed.

Challenges in the Sports Business

Without a doubt, sports is a difficult environment within which to work. I always try to communicate this to employment candidates. For me, it's imperative that I stress the particular difficulties of working within the demands of the New York Yankees. This organization is a pressure cooker due, in part, to the high demands of Yankees owner George Steinbrenner and the high visibility of the team in New York. When hiring for any sports position, it's essential that you accurately describe the working conditions whether the position is in the front office or on the field.

In today's world, all of sports involves pressure and high stakes. But in New York, the pressure is even more intense. Other cities may have one paper and one television station covering them; in New York we have anywhere from 8 newspapers covering the Yankees regularly and a dozen of television stations. New York, after all, is the media capital of the world. Without a doubt, New York, Boston, Philadelphia, and Tokyo, are the most scrutinized sports markets anywhere.

Taking the Lead in Media Relations

In the sports industry, there is never-ending public scrutiny fed by the media culture. Your success today is often only as good as the win or trade you made yesterday. As a GM, you must constantly explain your decisions not only to the owner and the fans but to the media as well.

Much like the CEO of a publicly traded company, a major league GM acts as the daily spokesman for the team. If a CEO errs in how he or she publicly represents a company, the reputation of the company – and the public's faith in it – may suffer. Likewise, if a GM represents the ball club or its members negatively, fan support can erode and a damaging firestorm might be created that could take weeks to extinguish.

As in any business – even in politics – it is essential that you have a strong media department. It has been said that having a good media relations department is like having a guardrail at the top of the mountain rather than an ambulance at the bottom. The most common scenario that you confront involves the breaking of a story. At first, there may be denial but ultimately the truth emerges. Damage control now becomes your focus; at that point, you may have already lost credibility and the trust of the media. It is far better to stay ahead of the story and to present the facts in your own words. In this way, you limit the amount of erroneous information attributed to you and your organization. When you are forthcoming with information, you also establish a great relationship with the media.

Personally, I adhere to the following four simple steps for developing successful media relationships:

• be honest
• be polite
• be prepared
• be aware

I cannot stress enough the importance of never lying – to the media, to the public, to the fan base. There is no law that dictates you must answer every question you are asked. If you don't want to answer a question at a particular moment in time you can always respond "no comment." Not responding is preferable to offering a misleading answer that can damage your credibility. Your goal should be to get out in front of issues rather than spend your time providing damage control. The best way to accomplish that is to be quick on your feet, smart, and honest.

What's Ahead

Since 1986, I have noticed that the baseball industry is employing more business practices and procedures. Today's baseball clubs are wiser when it comes to decision-making; they are more analytical. For example, during the past few years, much research has been conducted in the amateur draft arena. Many people have altered how they make draft decisions based on study results indicating that high school players, especially pitchers, come with significant risk. Projection of a player in this area is very difficult. In the past, teams have drafted a high rate in the first few rounds, with the most money being allocated to pitching. Studies have revealed that those are the riskiest drafts, yielding the highest percentage of players not actualizing their potential. We are seeing more of an emphasis in the upper portions of the draft: first, second, and third rounds are college-oriented players who are generally less risky. Because they have achieved more physical maturity, evaluating how these players might perform in the future isn't as difficult as it is with high school players.

Today's more analytical approach to baseball is positive for the entire industry. Owners look for more concrete reasons as to why and how they should spend their money. Nowadays, there must be fiscal analytical data to support the high salary purchases that are becoming more common.

In the future, I think baseball will develop and grow more internationally. Baseball has held exhibitions in Mexico and Japan; Italy may be next. Increasing the appeal of baseball abroad could open up untapped revenue streams.

There is also the possibility that China is planning to concentrate on the sport of baseball with the hope of attaining future success in the Olympics. This could be an exciting opportunity for baseball because with additional countries concentrating on baseball development, not only will more talent become available to the clubs, but certainly the love of our sport will grow and that translates into additional consumers.

Thoughts about the Field of Baseball

The best advice that I ever received – and the best that I can give – is this: Never lie to the media. In sports you are always on public display; it is essential that you never compromise yourself or your integrity. If the media has somehow ascertained a company secret and asks for a response, I will say "no comment" rather than lie about an issue. Misrepresenting a situation or providing misleading information can irreparably damage your reputation and that of your organization.

People are passionate about sports. And this passion results in an almost constant quest for information about a team and its players from the fan base. As GM I deal with the media on an ongoing basis. Newspaper reporters cover us daily. If you are looking to be in a business that generates a great deal of publicity, this is the perfect forum.

The baseball industry and sports in general are no different from a stock-driven company on Wall Street. As an organization you can live and die by your comments and by public perception. If I misrepresent this franchise in any way it can seriously impact the business side of our organization. It's imperative for me to clearly convey our direction and our vision in a way that is understandable and believable. In this way, I can help foster good relations with our fan base, which results in good business with our customers.

Fortunately, we don't have to use gimmicks, such as post-game concerts or fireworks, to entice people to come to the ballpark. Every year we have the same vision: for the Yankees to be the world champions. Since I became general manager in1998, we have won three World Series, five American League Championships, and six American League Eastern Division titles. We have been successful in fulfilling that vision.

I believe that your work and the passion you have for it reflect on you. Conducting yourself with integrity at all times is critical because you never know who is watching and how your behavior could impact your future. I believe, as do many people, that you see the same people going up the ladder as you see going down the ladder. It is important to treat everyone with respect.

Dick Williams, the manager of the Oakland A's when they won three world championships during the1970s, has an interesting story about the importance of treating people well. According to Williams, the two people on his championship team who became the most successful in life weren't players – they were the bat boy and the bat girl. The bat boy became the popular singer and performer MC Hammer; the bat girl became the creator of Mrs. Field's Cookies. Regardless of what position people hold in life, I believe it is incumbent on all of us to treat others as we, ourselves, would like to be treated.

Every individual who works in a position of authority, responsibility, and leadership faces difficult dilemmas, day in and day out. As a GM, I face the conflicts and the decisions common to environments where people have a passion for what they are doing. I believe that leading effectively

– in any organization – can occur only when you foster your own personal and professional development. Successful leadership depends on the knowledge and experience that is gained by embracing opportunities to learn and grow. Look for insights from those you admire and respect. In this way, your own personal growth, development, achievement, and success will never cease.

The New York Yankees are a successful business organization. And we have also been successful in providing our fan base with energy and entertainment, excitement and hope. Probably no one has a stadium large enough to fit all of the people who truly want to come and see one of our games. We are proud of our successes, to be sure. But we also take great pride in the fact that as a team, as a ball club, we have helped to fuel an enduring love for the game of baseball.

Entering his sixth season as General Manager of the New York Yankees, 35-year-old Brian McGuire Cashman is only the third GM in baseball history to win at least four consecutive League Championships and the first to do it in his first four seasons (1998-01). Only former Yankee General Manager Ed Barrow (four straight, 1936-39) and George Weiss (five straight, 1949-53) have also achieved the feat.

After serving five years as Assistant General Manager, Mr. Cashman was named General Manager of the Yankees on February 3, 1998. At 31 years old when promoted, Mr. Cashman became the second-youngest General Manager in baseball history (Randy Smith was 29 when named General Manager of the San Diego Padres on June 9, 1993). Upon winning the 1998 World Championship, he became the youngest GM to win a World Series, breaking the previous record held by the Minnesota Twins' Andy McPhail (33) in 1987. He went on to become the first GM to win three World Championships in his first three seasons.

In his first five seasons as General Manager, the Yankees have compiled a cumulative record of 497-309 – the best winning percentage (.617) in the Major Leagues during that period – and have appeared in post-season play each year, winning five consecutive AL East titles, four pennants and three World Championships. The Yankees earned ESPY awards – presented by ESPN – as "Outstanding Team of the Year" in 1998 and 2000 and they have also been named "Organization of the Year" by Baseball America in 1998 and USA Today in 1999. In addition, the Yankees established single-season franchise attendance records in 1998 (2,951,467), 1999 (3,292,736), and 2002 (3,465,807) and are the only New York sports franchise ever to top the three-million mark four times (1999-92).

Mr. Cashman joined the Yankees family as an intern in the Minor League and Scouting Department in June 1986 and, upon graduation from Catholic University in Washington, D.C. in June 1989, became a full-time Assistant in Baseball Operations. He was named Assistant General Manager, Baseball Administration on November 24, 1992 with responsibilities which included contract negotiations, player waivers, arbitration, budgeting and scheduling. He also served the club as Assistant Farm Director (1990-92).

Mr. Cashman attributes his quick rise through the organization to the direct tutelage he received from current and former General Manager's Bill Bergesch, Jim Bowden, Clyde King, Gene Michael, Bob Quinn, Brian Sabean, Syd Thrift, Bob Watson and Woody Woodward.

In 2001, Mr. Cashman received his third consecutive "40 Under 40 Award" presented by The Sports Business Journal, recognizing the top 40 people under the age of 40 who have made the greatest impact in the sports business industry. Mr. Cashman was also honored as the "Executive of the Year" in 2000 by the Boston Chapter of the BBWAA. He serves as Chairman of Major League Baseball's Rules Committee.

Born on July 3, 1967 in Rockville Center, NY, Mr. Cashman grew up in Lexington, KY. He attended Georgetown Prep in Rockville, MD, before attending Catholic University in Washington, D.C. to major in history and play intercollegiate baseball. His love for baseball developed when family friends (former Brooklyn Dodger) Ralph and Ann Branca arranged for him to serve as a bat boy for the Los Angeles Dodgers in spring training in 1982.

He and his wife, Mary, have a daughter, Grace Eva, born on 10/7/98.

An Insider's Look at – and Love for – Pro Basketball

Chris Wallace

General Manager
Boston Celtics

Business of Professional Sports

The business of professional sports has changed dramatically over the last decade or so because the stakes are so high financially for the team to operate. Payrolls are big; the commitment that you have to make to build stadiums is huge; it is all big business. It is more of a public business than any other business that you can imagine, with the exception of politics.

You can be the most successful real estate person in history, but there is no real estate talk radio. All of your moves are dissected. It is a tough balancing act because, obviously, every person who works for management in pro sports, or who owns a team, desperately wants to win a championship. But at the same time, you're trying to run a sound, financially responsible business. Those two can often be difficult and divergent goals to achieve.

The public, your consumer, does not care about your business. They just want to win and wonder why you are not signing the same guys the rivals are signing. Their idea of a good owner is not necessarily one who is running a business in a very sound, fiscally responsible way. That is what makes this a different business – very different from just about any other business you can think of.

I do not know the whole business model that other sports use. I know a little from a fan standpoint. I read about these issues in the paper. I know roughly the type of payroll and have some idea of their collective bargaining agreements with the players, but I do not know this inside and out. I really don't talk to people from these other sports; we're not likely to have social lunches and share details about our businesses.

Basketball, from my vantage point, is one of the healthiest pro sports, along with NFL football. We have cost certainty. We also have a mechanism in place that enables a team that drafts or comes up with a young player to have a very strong chance of retaining his services. That does not seem to be the case in baseball.

For example, we drafted Paul Pierce in 1998. On a rookie scale, you can extend a player's contract after three years. The fourth year is very advantageous. You can expect it after the third; also, up until October 31st of the third year, you also can trigger the fourth year. You then have him on the roster for four years. After the third year, you can extend the contract; you can give him up to six additional years; and since he is already on the books for year four, it actually means seven years. The earliest he can negotiate with outside teams is after the fourth year. At that point he is a restricted free agent.

Let's say the player detests his situation and desperately wants out to go to a team closer to home. If he wanted to wait through the whole process, he would be a totally unrestricted free agent after the fifth year. After the fourth, we can match it. In a vast majority of cases, the coveted young player just re-ups with his old team after the third year. It makes sense, and we can also pay him more. We can give him a 12.5 percent raise, and the outside teams can give him 10 percent. We can start off at a higher number, and he can get that security early, rather than waiting for the fourth year. You just have a tremendous home field advantage in retaining your young players. That makes it easier for a small- to mid-market team to be highly successful – San Antonio, for example.

I don't know how football works. I know you have to get under a hard cap every year. Let's say Tim Duncan was a baseball player and Paul Pierce was a baseball player. The Yankees and the Dodgers would be right on our necks poaching our play. We would not have any advantage. We would not be able to give them a contract at an earlier date. We wouldn't even be able to pay them more necessarily. I think basketball is a much more controlled situation.

General Manager's Role

I am the team's general manager. I used to be the top basketball executive; now Danny Ainge is. I still do many of the same things. I scout the new talents that are available every year in the draft. I oversee the minor league coverage, and I scout European players for the draft and free agents, either European players who have gone through the draft unselected or American players who were abroad and want to come home. I talk to other teams about trade negotiations. I work with the agents on contact negotiations. I also spend a great deal of time interacting with ownership to let them know what I'm doing. I work together with ownership on the team's short and long-term plans and I deal with the media.

There is some interaction with the players, and some talks that happen from time to time, but I'm not out there every day giving pep talks to the players. The final aspect is I deal with the NBA league office. There are certain things I have to file for them and requirements throughout the year and paperwork. Some of my role is dealing with these requirements.

I don't run the business side of the Celtics. The business side is run from 151 Merrimac, across the street from the Fleet Center. The basketball operations headquarters is in Waltham. I do not have day-to-day responsibilities for the business side. I think that is how you would see most teams set up. I would say my duties as a general manager are pretty similar to those of another team's GM.

The big difference was probably over the last couple of years. I was never given complete control of the basketball operation. Rick Pitino was in control of it until he left, and afterwards, Jim O'Brien and I were equal; neither of us was the other's superior. That is different than how most teams establish a chain of command.

Coaching, Chemistry, and Competitive Spirit

Danny Ainge is here and in charge of basketball operations, and he has the final say. But it is very much a collaborative, collective effort. NBA teams do not have large staffs compared to other sports or to most businesses. There are only twelve to fifteen players on a team. Unlike baseball, we are not permitted to sign teenage free agents from abroad. We are not in a race with the Knicks for the next great young fifteen-year-old player in Yugoslavia. We have to go through a draft process.

This whole talent acquisition process starts from the premise that the NBA is a talent league. It is the ultimate talent league because of the sheer math of the game. You have only ten players on the court at one time – under half of the personnel on a football field at one time. We have twelve to fifteen people on a roster; baseball has twenty-five, and football is in the fifties. So one player makes a much greater difference in the game of basketball.

The NBA game is also eight minutes longer than a college game. Our shot clock is eleven seconds shorter. We play 82 regular season and 8 preseason games – three times a normal college schedule, and that is not counting the playoffs. There are so many more possessions in an average NBA game and over the course of a season.

The difference that one player makes is so dramatic. You can't monkey with the game in the NBA as you can in college by slowing the game down. In college basketball, for example, the top team that wins the National Championship goes to the head of the selection process. They have an easier time coming up with the top high school players. If you win the championship in the NBA, you draft in the late 20s.

In the ultimate talent league, you need good coaching and good chemistry. You need all of these intangibles, and I don't want to underestimate them, but if you don't have the players, it doesn't make a difference how strong your intangibles are. We are trying to gauge the talent level of these players and how much of an impact they can make. In the draft in particular, because we are dealing with so many more foreign players and young players – we drafted a player from high school – than ever before, the draft has become a futures market. Teams certainly want an immediate impact from the players they pick, but they also don't want to miss on a Kobe Bryant, a Tracy McGrady, a Kevin Garnett.

We are dealing with younger players. We are dealing with many more prospects between the ages of eighteen and twenty than ever before. When I got into the NBA in 1986, we were looking only at college players. In a few cases there were some underclassmen, who were almost always juniors. The only players who came out after their sophomore year were the truly great ones, like a Magic Johnson or Isaiah Thomas or a few players who had some off-the-court problems or were in trouble academically and had to leave school.

Obviously if you are watching players over four years and trying to evaluate them at the age of twenty-one or twenty-three, you have an easier process than dealing with younger players. You lack the comparative element that was so prevalent in the past where you could see all of these guys in great college programs. There were two guys selected in the first round this year from Yugoslavia who played on a team that was 2-14 in the EuroLeague and lost games by fifty to seventy points. If one guy played eighteen minutes, it was a big night for him. A third player was drafted and played one minute, thirty-three seconds in a game in Yugoslavia I scouted.

The attraction of the young players, however, is their talent level. Even though these guys don't have the statistics and experience of American college seniors, they are commodities because of their talent level. Also, many international players have fared well in recent years, and the same goes for high school players. When you are evaluating a high school player for a draft, and he is in a high school game, there is a pretty good chance there is nobody on the court who could compete with him, so he is not being pushed by any stretch of the imagination. You have to fill in the blanks.

On the list of the all-stars in the league, or on the All-Pro team – the top fifteen guys – many didn't go through four years of college. You have Kevin Garnett, Tracy McGrady, Kobe Bryant, and Jermaine O'Neil. They are all on the All-Pro team and didn't even go to college. Then you have Dirk Nowitzki, who is an international player, and many players who were in college for only one or two years, like Jason Kidd.

It is not that we aren't going to draft a four-year guy because we don't think he has any upside, but the top young kids today, both from abroad and the United States, by and large, are not making it to college. In Europe, the equivalent of a college senior is twenty-two, so they are eligible to be drafted when they are twenty-two, unless they declare early for the draft. These elite players are not waiting to twenty-two to enter the draft. Our best players domestically are not going through four years of college today. There is less to judge them on. You have to fill in the blanks and use your imagination more than before.

When you look at the trends and what groups the top players of the world are coming from, you see that they are coming from ranks other than college seniors. It broadens our scope. We have some advantages in this field in that there is so much intersectional play in the United States. The top high school players play in the AAU tournaments, and then they go on to college. So Stanford is playing Boston College, and Miami is playing Ohio State, and you get to see them in numerous competitive environments. Over the course of a few years, they sort themselves out to a certain degree.

The other thing is the top young players in our game, the elite players, are easily identifiable when they are teenagers. I have a saying that if a guy is going to be great, you should be able to go to a game, and know it in five to ten minutes. He should just knock you out. If you are a theatergoer and see the great actors and all-time Broadway performances, it just knocks you out. It's like that in basketball. They have the size and athletic ability, and all of these things are easily identifiable. That is an advantage we have that I don't think they necessarily have in baseball. In football they have to comb through more players than we do, and there are more guys from the outer reaches who can become stars. We don't have Tom Bradys in the NBA by and large.

It is talent first. If a guy is going to be great, he will have to have several things in line. He has to have talent, sufficient size, and athleticism that matches up with his position, productivity, and a resume you can fall back on. Then he'll have to have intangibles – an insatiable desire to compete and dominate. If you have all of those elements in line, then you may have a great player.

For your support people, generally you are looking for one or two NBA elements to their game. It could be shot blocking, rebound, scoring, shooting, and so on. You are not asking that player to possess every skill. Strong intangibles and a tremendous sense of perseverance are very helpful with those types of players because often they will be under-appreciated and have to kick around a while before they find a home in the NBA.

We have Mark Blount on our team who is in his fourth year in the NBA. He was cut six times by NBA teams, foreign teams, and American minor league teams before we got him. He had a legitimate center size. He was very athletic and ran the floor well for someone that size. He was extremely humble because he had been tossed out the door so many times. His professional career was not going as he expected, and we caught him at just the right time.

Those situations take a little more examination. To watch LeBron James play and come to the conclusion that he can be a great player, you don't have to be a great talent evaluator.

We can add players through the draft. You seldom have more than three draft picks in one year. You only have two rounds with 58 selections in an NBA draft. If you hit with the draft just every couple of years, it is a tremendous boon for your franchise because these players are on a rookie scale contract, which is very advantageous to the team. For example, with Paul Pierce, you have a tremendous home court advantage when it comes to re-signing. We can also do trades. We can trade for other players and draft choices. I look at the draft as a free shot because the only complications are that X number of players will be taken off the board when you come up. At that point you can take anyone – you don't have to worry about salary cap ramifications or making a trade with another team. It's all on you.

Trading becomes more complex and difficult to pull off because you have to get another team or two to tango with you. The deal has to work under the trading salary cap rules. It has to be a deal that is acceptable to the other team. You don't shove things down people's throats in this business. The financial ramifications of our deals are all well known. All teams have the salary sheets and know what the players earn. You're not commandeering some obscure piece of real estate whose value is not known. When you make that trade, it has to pass the litmus test that it makes sense afterward for the teams. It should make sense both financially and as far as PR is concerned. Nobody wants to do a trade where they'll get killed by the media and the fans. So when you throw all of those elements into the blender, it is hard to come up with a trade. There are many variables you don't control.

In free agency, you have to have either the cap room to sign big-time free agents or use salary exceptions each team has at its disposal. We have a Million Dollar Exception and a Midlevel Exception worth close to $5M. Free agency is a little like college recruiting. You can go out and woo a player; you have to convince him your situation works for him. If he is a small forward, and you already have three small forwards who are good, he probably won't want to come play for you. Maybe he is from California and wants to go closer to home. Or you can be out-bid by the Knicks or the Lakers. You don't control that, either.

The one thing you do control, other than the draft, is signing these minimum salary players and bringing guys out of the CBA and players who come back from Europe. With those players, it is always first come, first served: They go where the initial offer is.

As you can see, we have a limited number of vehicles to bring in new talent. We go to the plate, to use a baseball metaphor, fewer times a season than our counterparts do in the other pro sports because our volume is so much lower.

This is an inexact science. If you take the rosters of any NBA team and look at their contracts and compare them, nobody has a perfect roster. Every team will have some tremendous guys, players who are doing very well and over-producing, and everyone will have some under-producing players. Many times when you have players whose contracts are on the high side, you will see that teams were backed into a corner. There was no one else at that time to fill a particular position or need.

Let's say they felt one player could make a difference in getting into the playoffs or reaching the conference finals. We unfortunately are in a business where there is a scarcity of talent. The well is not overflowing with players who can make a difference over the long haul in the NBA. There are large numbers of players who can be on a team, but very few who can make a difference. So the supply and demand factor doesn't work in your favor.

Basically, you sit down with your ownership, get the parameters, and do the best you can to keep the contracts reasonable in your contract negotiations, so to not leave yourself too exposed. I think there are a lot fewer long-term contracts in the league now for the non-elite players than there were when I came to Boston. You limit your exposure as best as possible. You try to compare each player and his role as you perceive it on your team with other similar players around the league. I can't stress enough that contract negotiations are an inexact science.

Obviously our most important hires are our players. Second are the coaches. I've never actually hired a coach. Jim O'Brien and I came in together, and that has worked out wonderfully; he has done a tremendous job. On the other side of the hiring question as far as scouts and support people are concerned, we have a small staff. There hasn't been a great deal of hiring during the seven years I have been with the Celtics. But if I did have a hiring philosophy, it would be to try to find people who are smarter and more talented than I am.

The Extra Kick from Rivalries

From our standpoint, I believe the Nets are a rival. They beat us two years ago, and they swept us in the playoffs last year. I don't know what their perspective is. I think they are one of our main rivals. The 76ers are also a pretty big rival, since we faced them in the playoffs a few years ago. And the rivalries with New York and the Los Angeles Lakers go back several decades.

Rivalries are extremely important. You have to have a team to hate for your fans. It adds that extra kick – for example, the Red Sox/Yankees rivalry. You don't have to be much of a baseball fan to sit on the periphery and see how important that is to people and the type of media coverage it receives. In NFL football you have rivalry between the Patriots and the Jets.

The Celtics have probably had more strong and heated rivalries than any other team in the NBA.

Community Ties Are Crucial

The only reason there is professional sports today is the interest of the fans. If there wasn't tremendous interest in all of these teams, then we would be croquet. We don't have to worry about being evangelists in getting the word out and selling the need for our service to people, as so many businesses have to, because it already exists. People relate to what you have, and there is tremendous free media coverage.

Pro sports have some major advantages that other businesses don't have. Something else we have that most businesses don't have is tremendous scrutiny by the public. We have to get out with our fans and interact with them as much as possible. We have to get our players out there, which this team does. We have to get them into the community, shaking hands and supporting charitable causes. This contact is important because we are in an era where unfortunately so much of the business of pro sports has seeped into the front page of the paper, especially the attention given to the salaries our players earn. There have been some very acrimonious situations in cities in terms of getting public funding for new arena and stadium construction.

We also have player conduct issues that lap over to the front page of the paper. So the sports fan over the last ten to twenty years has been subjected to much greater controversy than fans of earlier eras. When fans decide to become emotionally attached and support individual teams, they spend their discretionary income and their time on sports. Having players involved in the community helps maintain that tie.

You also need your front office people, your ownership, and your coaches involved in community affairs, but they don't have the visibility of your players. You get your players out there so people realize they are good guys and that they care. Yes, they do make a lot of money, but they love what they are doing, and they are worth supporting. That is huge.

We are involved in all sorts of functions and affairs. Our community affairs division has won awards. We have players reading at schools and running basketball clinics in the off-season. We are involved in the "Stay in School" program, where students who have perfect attendance come to an assembly at Northeastern University in May and get certificates and enjoy entertainment. We also have a great program on game day called "Heroes Among Us," where they bring in someone who has made an especially notable contribution to the community and honor them. We have had firefighters, average people who have rescued others, educators – a wide assortment of people.

Revenue Matters

In the NBA we have our gates and our ticket sales, both single games and season tickets. Season ticket sales are the backbone of our teams. We have our local radio and television contracts. We have the national television contracts that are negotiated by the NBA. Teams with their own arenas have signage. We have the luxury boxes, though again you usually have to own your own arena to have that. Concessions and parking come with owning your own arena. The Celtics do not own the Fleet Center, although there has been a tremendous explosion in teams building their own arenas in the last decade. We have our souvenir sales

– jerseys, caps, T-shirts, and so on – as a revenue source. The major revenues come from national TV, local media, and ticket sales.

The single biggest thing a team can do to increase its profits is to have an exciting, successful team. Some people in sports marketing feel you can market almost anything through sound sales and marketing principles. Maybe they're right; I'm not an expert on sports marketing. But I see a definite correlation when you go around the league, that the most successful and exciting teams draw the best. They are on television more than the teams that aren't as appealing. That, I think, is the greatest gift you can give to the franchise – creating that type of winning team.

Success in Tradition: They Will Come

What dictates success is basically winning games. Each individual ownership has its own financial parameters. Whether those parameters are high or low, on the overall league scale, the determining factor is still winning. Sometimes there is a personality rift with ownership or between coaches and players. Most often, if you win, you stay; if you lose, you don't.

We all strive to achieve a championship, but you have to be realistic. In the NBA seldom does a team go from nowhere to a championship overnight. That can happen in football. It does not seem to happen frequently in baseball.

Winning is generally a gradual process in the NBA, where you have to get into the playoffs and experience the pain and learn from that to move up the ladder. I think we're still in that process. I am happy, considering where we were just a few short years ago, which we often lose sight of. When Rick Pitino left in January 2001, we were given up for dead. Since then, the Celts are well over .500 and have been in the playoffs two of those three years. We were second, behind the Nets, over the last two years in playoff wins for the Eastern Conference. So I think a great deal has been accomplished.

The Celtics have a tremendous brand name. We have the most impressive legacy and the richest history of all the NBA franchises. Our sixteen NBA championships are more than any other franchise can boast. Red Auerbach, our patriarch, is one of the all-time great coaches and front office executives. We had Bill Russell, the greatest defensive player ever to play basketball, and Larry Bird, one of the top ten players in the history of the game. We have had some of the all-time greatest "sixth men." The list goes on and on.

We are also fortunate to be located in a sports-intensive hot spot – not just Boston, but all of New England. I came here from a Sun Belt city. There is a major difference in the fever of the fans and the intensity of the media coverage here, in New York, and in Philadelphia, from what you feel in Sun Belt cities. They don't have the legacy of intense interest being passed down from father to son. I worked for the Miami Heat, which was an expansion team. No one in Miami ever said to me that they remember going to playoff games in 1963 with their father.

Tradition makes the business end of the operation much easier to run successfully. We have tradition, fans, and very extensive and intensive media coverage in Boston. So if you do anything at all, they will come. You don't have to have the best team in the league or be champion-bound – you just have to have hope. Your team has to play hard and show there is a chance, and the fans will come in Boston. That is not the case in every city.

The demographics here help, also. This area is one of the leading markets in the country and one of the more affluent overall metropolitan areas in the nation. You have very good media contracts here, with radio and television. I am not on the business side, but I can tell you that this is a very attractive place to do sports business. That provides a team with a tremendous advantage.

This team has been well run on the business side and in terms of financial planning. It was a profitable entity under the Gaston family. While they have only been in charge of the team since December 31, 2002, Boston Basketball Partners LLC is very hands on, local, and successful in their own individual occupations. They bring a tremendous amount of business experience and acumen to this process. They are fans. They have continued to run the team well on the business side, and I think we will get stronger as the years go by and they pick up more experience.

Boston is right up there among the elite cities for sports, right beside New York, Chicago, and Philadelphia. Los Angeles doesn't have a football team now. Dallas seems to do well; they have successful teams and the population base to support them. I am sure I am missing some cities, but this is about as strong as it gets.

The Future: Competition Everywhere

We did a four-year plan in April 2001. We have met many of those expectations so far. Obviously, our primary goal is to win a championship, but we can't just say to ourselves that we're going to sit around here and do nothing until we get a championship. Steps have to be taken. Not every move you make is one that necessarily inches you toward a championship. You make moves for the short term, as well, to give you the ability to compete in a shorter window. Our goal is to win a title. We want to have an exciting, entertaining team that is very well received by fans, so that we have strong attendance at the Fleet Center, and the television ratings are high. It is important for ownership groups to be fiscally responsible.

You can't look at every move an NBA team could make and say it would bring you a title or bring you closer to a title. The majority of moves are made to make you as good as you can be right now. We are in an instant-gratification society now. You can go out and talk to civic groups and tell the media that we are here to win a title and that everything is geared around that, which it is. But you also have to give people some hope in the short term. You have to entertain them and win some games, or you will have nobody riding the bandwagon with you. That is not given a lot of attention, but I understand it very clearly from being in Boston the last six years.

You often read about teams in the NBA that say they are going to shed salary and get way down under the cap. They won't be that concerned with the short term, and they want to get some young players to build for a championship. That sounds good, but during that period between your announcement and reaching the team's objective, when you realistically can compete for a title, you may be wandering through an NBA desert for many seasons.

What I have found is that it is almost impossible during the down times to keep management, ownership, fans, and media all on the same page. Those groups will jump off your bandwagon at different times. Eventually, you may have a bandwagon with nobody on it because winning a title just looks too far away. The short term can be brutal if the team is not winning.

The ownership is the most important group to please. If you are in my position, you are held accountable by your ownership. You answer to ownership. If you are going to continue to work in this field down the road, other owners will be the ones to hire you. Basically that is who you answer to – the choir you are preaching to.

No one knows, for example, what type of economic climate we are walking into. The world has changed so much on all fronts during the last decade, particularly the last two years. Who knows what our world will be? That will dictate to a great degree a lot of player acquisitions we can do outside of the draft.

It is impossible to forecast the tastes of the consumer over the next decade or two – their buying habits, their leisure habits. For example, in just the brief period of time that I have been in the NBA – it seems like a long time, but it has only been sixteen years – HBO hasn't always been nearly the factor it is now. There was no *Sex in the City* and these other hit HBO shows. You didn't have the proliferation of various forms of satellite television. You can sit at home right now and watch more than 300 channels. The Internet was practically not in existence. There are so many more options for people to spend their entertainment dollar and their leisure time than ever before. So we can't, right now, forecast the trends that will give us advantages in how we are perceived by the public or make it more difficult for us to drum up a fan base. Those are the truly challenging questions.

Even though I am not involved in the business side of our operations, we all answer to the financial realities of the team. It entirely shapes out the future. We have been so lucky in pro sports that we have lived through a golden era, and there has been an unlimited supply of fan interest. Hopefully that will continue in the future. I am speaking of the industry as a whole. We are in an age in which, because of the technology and the world growing so much smaller, things change at a much more rapid rate. Hopefully, professional sports can keep pace with that changing world.

For the Love of the Game

I had Billy Cunningham, who is a member of the Basketball Hall of Fame, tell me that if you listen to the fans, you will end up sitting in the stands with them. That is an interesting comment. I believe that today, we have to interact with the fans and listen to their opinions, but I don't believe we have to do everything they desire in terms of player acquisitions. I do believe we have to respect the commitment they are making with their time and money.

It would make things easier if the public and the media could see these players and coaches in the light in which we see them. We have the luxury to be around them to a much greater degree. Often the money side of pro sports overshadows the competitive nature and the quality of the people involved. I believe many players, in the eyes of some of the fans and the media, walk around with their contracts on the backs of their jerseys, rather than their numbers. I wish there was a way we could separate that part of the business from the pure aspect of playing.

When basketball is all distilled down to its simplest elements, these are men playing a little boy's game – the little boy's game they grew up playing and loved to play, and still love to play today. Unfortunately, that passion is often obscured. Our players in the NBA work hard. From the time they start camp at the beginning of October to the end of the season in April, May, or June, there are almost no off days. Although we fly around in private planes and stay at great hotels, it takes tremendous physical and emotional tolls, on not only our players, but on our coaches as well. The schedule is extremely arduous. I wish the fans and the media could get to know these people better. I think that would make all of our jobs a lot easier.

This is a tremendous way to earn a living. If you are interested in sports, there is nothing like working on the sports side of a pro team. This beats anything else that I have ever done, and I've had a number of occupations. There is an immediacy to our results that is not always there in other businesses. You win and lose these games very quickly, so it doesn't take four or five years to notice growth and change. You are truly under a bright – and at times, very harsh – light. But it is a thrill to compete and try to build something. We all get very handsomely paid for it. It has been a great, great way to make a living for me. There is no way I can approximate it outside this industry, either in the personal satisfaction or the financial rewards.

One of the foremost evaluators of basketball talent, Chris Wallace is entering his seventh season as General Manager of the Boston Celtics. Wallace has been instrumental in the formation of the young and talented Celtics roster with a number of trades, free agent signings, and solid draft choices. His basketball expertise and savvy will continue to be critical to the future development of the franchise.

Wallace was Director of Player Personnel for the Miami Heat before coming to Boston. The Heat won a franchise-record 61 games in 1996-97, and Wallace is credited with discovering many of the Heat's players. His responsibilities included college and international scouting and searching for potential talent in the CBA as well as the NBA. Wallace was promoted to that position after four extremely successful years as a scout for the Heat.

Before joining the Heat, Wallace worked in various scouting capacities for the Portland Trail Blazers, Denver Nuggets, Los Angeles Clippers, and New York Knicks. He also worked as a draft consultant for the United States Basketball League. Wallace served on the selection committee for the prestigious Nike/ABCD and Converse ABCD national high school camps evaluating scores of future college and NBA stars.

In 1981, Wallace founded the award-winning Blue Ribbon College Basketball Yearbook, his first venture into the basketball business. Sports Illustrated named Wallace as one of the most influential members of the college basketball media in 1991. He has also served as an expert witness in basketball-related litigation.

Investing in the Future of Soccer

Jim Smith

General Manager
Columbus Crew

Soccer and the Business of Sport

The real business of sports is to provide an entertainment outlet that allows fans and members of the community to go out and enjoy an evening and watch the highest-level athletes participate in competition. If we can provide a fun, entertaining, cost-effective atmosphere as part of that, that's a very competitive product. The bottom line is that ultimately we are driven to make money, like any business, but while we do that we provide a valuable asset to the community.

The business of soccer is driven by two primary revenue streams: ticket sales and sponsorship revenue. Maximizing those revenue streams while maintaining costs is what will provide the most successful formula for a professional soccer team. When you can add in the ancillary revenues from a stadium that you can control or negotiate a good deal with, that can only make your business better. In our case, we control the ancillary revenues at Crew Stadium, and that's why we are, as of now, the most successful professional soccer franchise in this country. In our case, our ownership group built our own stadium. That required an enormous investment, but by providing a state-of-the-art facility for professional soccer, we were able to control all the revenue streams.

There is one clear difference between soccer and every other professional sport, and that is the absence of television revenue. Right now we don't share in any of the television revenue from a team perspective, and that is the major difference between us and the other four major professional sports. The other significant difference is that our ticket prices are still considerably lower on average than those for the other four sports as well. Thus, considering both of those things, our overall revenue streams are smaller. Until we are able to grow those revenue streams, we're going to be behind the other four professional sports.

I think the one big advantage that we have is that all ten teams in the MLS are extremely competitive, and on any given day any team can beat the other team. That creates major fan excitement and major interest all the way through the season, because every game is compelling and no team is ever out of the playoff hunt. The downside to that is that we're not in enough markets to gather enough national appeal to really push us over the tipping point of popularity. Expansion needs to happen in order to get us more eyeballs and more attention in the media in other markets outside our ten core markets.

The long-term vision of the MLS is to be in the top five soccer leagues in the world – and I think we're making some fairly good progress – both on and off the field. Our quality of play has gone up significantly and our business has gotten better, whereas the business of soccer around the world has really leveled off except for the English Premier League and the German Bundesliga and maybe a couple of others.

The Fans

Ohio was a very good soccer state, and the community really embraced being one of the first Major League Soccer markets to be announced in our country. The reception by the fans was overwhelming from the start. This team has been near the top of the league in seven out of eight years in season-ticket sales, which is probably the key indicator of core fans for a professional sports team. This organization has done an excellent job developing the brand in this marketplace and really carving its niche with fans and generating interest in the Crew in what is really an OSU Buckeye community.

From the very beginning, the team has truly been a part of this community. And I believe that for any team to be successful it has to be a part of the fabric of the community. Players have to feel that they live in this community and give back to the community. I think this team has made it its mantra to really be a part of this community – making public appearances, being accessible to the fans, and developing a good motto of being "America's Hardest-Working Team." I think that kind of work ethic slogan carried onto the field with the players, but really resonated with the fans in Columbus because they really respect the hard work that goes in day to day. If you put a hard day's work in, I think that Midwesterners value that.

We are among the few professional sports team in this country to continue to sign autographs. Our players sign autographs after every game, and I think that sends a clear message that we value our fans. Win or lose, after every game, players go through what we have called "Autograph Alley." On a rainy day it will only be hundreds, but on a warm summer night it will be thousands of people – adults and children alike – waiting for autographs after a game and appreciating the effort put out on the field, and the guys appreciating the fans in the stands.

Outside the game, we continue to do clinics in the community for young soccer players. Throughout the community, we continue to make appearances and are very involved in charitable causes of all kinds, particularly child-related causes. We do a number of public service announcements and support causes through PSAs. So I think our players have a good profile in supporting charities that are important to our own community.

If you came to a game you would see that there are quite a few fans who are intense and very passionate about soccer. You develop that over time. It also helps to treat your fans well and really give them a quality product to root for and have them identify with the players. Getting to really know and understand our players creates a little bit more passion for our team. Another way the sport will grow in passion is that as it gets more media attention and is in more markets, more rivalries will be created. If you come to a game between the Columbus Crew and the Chicago Fire, you would see incredible passion and some downright hatred between fans. The same thing with the Crew and DC United. DC United knocked the Crew out of the playoffs the first three years, and DC United won two or three championships in those first three years. So, there is some pretty good passion and rivalry established in a very young league, and I think that will continue to evolve as this league continues to progress.

The number-one most important thing for us is our fans – taking care of our fans and making sure our fans not only have a good experience when they come to a game, but that the customer service for the fans is at its absolute best. We always drive to provide the highest level of customer service to our season-ticket holders, group buyers, individual game buyers, and just fans in general.

Running the Team

As president and general manager, I oversee the entire operation of our business, which includes the stadium and the team – both from the players' side and the business side. We have one executive vice president and two vice presidents all overseeing different parts of our business. The coach reports directly to me, and all our player/personnel decisions ultimately run through me as well.

Managing a workforce of athletes is interesting; their needs are very different from those of a normal work staff. You want to provide an environment that helps them to be at their best all the time, every day, from training to games. Creating that environment can be very difficult. And you have to manage the expectations of these players in terms of what is feasible while providing them absolutely everything you can to give them the best advantage to win games. You have to create an environment of success, so they can be champions. You need to give them all the resources, and that means great coaches, great facilities, the support of the organization. All those things have to be there in order for us to be successful.

Because we own our own stadium, our organization looks different from most. In addition, we are a self-contained unit. We do all our own sponsorship sales; we don't outsource any of it. We do all our own ticket sales and operations. Other teams either rent the stadium, so they don't have any stadium personnel, or the stadium personnel don't report to the president/general manager. I think we're the most integrated soccer business in this country, and I think that's the right way to go about it. I think it's probably why we we've been the most successful. We're not sharing any resources with another professional sports team, with another outside entity, or with a stadium. We are a self-contained unit and we run efficiently. But we also run with the big picture in mind, which is to continue to grow our business, our revenue streams. And I think we're able to do that because everything is under one leader.

There's no question that the team owning the stadium helps, because all the players feel like this is their permanent home. We're not playing in a rented building; this is our locker room – it looks like our locker room, and these are our team colors. You don't feel like a tenant, or that you're just showing up at the stadium to play a game. I think the guys respect not only our facility but our business a little bit more because they know that our owners put the investment in to build our own place.

There is another model that has been successful as well: when an NFL team has owned a Major League Soccer team and has shared resources. I think from the standpoint of reducing expenses, that's probably a pretty efficient way to go. I don't know, though, if it's the best way to grow your business to get it to where it ultimately needs to be. Those are two schools of thought.

In every company there's always a pressure to increase revenue and reduce expenses. I don't think we're any different. We run into the same management challenges of finding quality personnel to fit within a budget that makes your business and the model work. We're a little less dependent on the market, but clearly the economy factors into our ultimate business because discretionary income is what people spend on entertainment. So if there is less discretionary income, that will negatively affect our business. We're competing with other entertainment options, and we have to make ourselves more attractive when there is a shrinking discretionary dollar.

One way to grow revenues is to increase ticket prices. The other is to increase sales. It's a pretty basic formula for us. More ticket sales and a little bit higher prices raise our revenues every year. And that is what we continue to try to do: slightly raise prices and sell more tickets – and sell more sponsorship. We've had a very good run on sponsorship lately, and that will impact our overall profitability more than anything else.

Last year we won the U.S. Open Cup Tournament championship. We have Brian McBride, who is probably one of the top three most recognizable soccer players in this country. He's a great individual and has been with this team for eight years; he's a star. So, we have a championship, we have our own facility, we have marquee player; this clearly helps our business. If we win the MLS Cup (league championship) this year, would it help us increase our revenue streams? I'd say yes, but not as dramatically as it does in other sports.

One risk that we deal with is that some players warrant a guaranteed salary. Our model is very similar to the NFL model in which players' contracts are a series of one-year options. There are some players in our league who have guaranteed contracts, so it's automatic. You sign a three-year deal and they're on your books for three years. If that player gets hurt, they're still on your books. So that's one of the inherent risks that you have; you can sign a player to a guaranteed contract, they can get hurt and you're stuck with their salary on your salary cap. Also, they may not perform as well as you had anticipated and they're still stuck on your salary. You run the risk of signing players to guaranteed contracts; that's an inherent risk on the player side.

Defining Success

I think we're already the best professional soccer organization in this country. We want to be mentioned as being one of the best professional soccer organizations in the world. One of the ways we do that is through continuing to lead in our own country. As long as we're always in the hunt with Los Angeles, New York, Boston, and Philadelphia for men's and women's national team games, we'll always be at the top of the game. For us, being the smallest venue to be selected for the 2003 Women's World Cup continues to reinforce the fact that we're doing an excellent job from an organization standpoint and that we are one of the model organizations in this country for soccer. Continuing to be in that position is extremely important.

We want to win a championship every year. That's an on-the-field goal every year. We also want to lead the league in paid attendance every year. We want to lead the league in sponsorship revenue every year, even though we're the smallest market. I qualify market size by the television ranking, so we're smaller than Kansas City.

A good business plan is critical. The number-one revenue variable year in and year out is ticket sales. You need a plan to continue to grow your season-ticket sales, but also to continue to grow your individual game ticket sales. The one factor that could influence it the most and that we have absolutely no control over is weather; we don't have rain-outs in soccer. So if it's bad weather, or has been bad weather leading up to game time, that will directly affect the number of tickets sold and the number of people who show up to the game. When you control your own revenue streams, having people show up is as important as having people buy the tickets, because of that extra revenue that we're losing if they're no-shows. There aren't a lot of same-day ticket buyers, but they can make the difference between making budget and not making budget. We have a budgeted number that we anticipate every game that will walk up and buy a ticket the day of the game. It might be 10 percent of our overall ticket buyers. It's not huge, but it still makes a difference in the overall revenue model. We certainly hope to get to a day where that won't be a factor. If I can be sold out going into every game and not have to worry about weather or whether we're going to do any walk-up sales that day, that's the ideal setting we want to get to.

To ensure the team's future success, you try not to get caught up too much in the short term; you're always looking at the long term. I don't think there are too many of us who look 100 years down the road; I think most of us look five to 10 years down the road and try to assess how our decisions today are going to impact that going forward. Our league, because it's only eight years old, looks at it a bit differently than the NFL may. We're looking at milestones of 5 to 10 years and making sure that we're making decisions that will be in line with where we're going to be 5 to 10 years from now. From our player/personnel decisions to our salary cap to our business practices, all need to be in line not just for today but for the years to come.

What we need to do to really make sure that we're going to continue to be part of this community and to be successful in this community long term is to make sure that we never lose sight of what's important for our own community, which is being involved – being active, positive members of our society. I think the NHL team in town has done an excellent job at that; clearly, for eight years, we've done a very good job at that. We always try to be out in front supporting community initiatives and really promoting the fact that the community comes first and the team may come second. I use the example of bringing the World Cup qualifying games, in which the U.S. and Mexico played, here on February 28. It was 31 degrees at kick-off and we had standing room only: 24,000-plus people here in attendance at the stadium, screaming. The NHL Blue Jackets were sold out downtown with another 18,000 crowd. Professional soccer continues to put Columbus on the map because we do very well with these high-profile soccer events. By continuing to do that for the community and giving the community a little bit of a higher profile, I think that's part of what our organization has to do to remain successful. We need to continue to do that 5 and 10 years down the road.

The Blue Jackets coming in has not been a negative development for the Crew. I think from a business standpoint, we compete in different seasons. We complement from a pricing standpoint; we're a mid-point, they're probably a high-end. From a sponsor standpoint, we compete very well because we're a different price point and we deliver what I think is a more attractive audience: adults 18–34 and families 25–54. I think our demographics are very attractive for sponsors, and that's continuing to bear out as we've had our third consecutive year of record sponsorship sales.

The Players

For us, two things go into assessing the value of a player: Clearly, what we think of the player overall and what position the player plays, but probably the biggest factor in what we can afford to pay a player will have to do with our own salary cap. We have a hard cap in Major League Soccer – a finite number of dollars to work with. Every player thinks he deserves more money, but in reality some players might actually be worth more than what we're paying them. All we can do is offer what we have in the salary cap. We try to put the best team together based on the parameters of salary cap, and that's the biggest challenge. Players have an option to not sign and go somewhere else, but that's where the tangible value of having a stadium, your own training site, and the best fan base in Major League Soccer all factor in to a player's decision to maybe take a little less money to stay in Columbus versus a little more money to play somewhere else.

If the players are that good, then we should be winning championships. This year we have four players who are on their respective national teams right now. We've had Brian McBride, who has been in the league for all eight years, and who has been on loan and has played overseas. This year he's made the decision to come back and play for Columbus because it's a great place to play and he likes living in the United States.

In the past, players have left other leagues to play in the MLS only at an older age, so a player may be on the downside of a career and wants to finish in the MLS. We don't do that as much anymore. Is David Beckham ever going to play in the MLS while he's in his prime? No. Our league is just not set up to the point where we're going to pay ungodly salaries when the revenue streams don't support it.

There is a draft in the MLS. There aren't farm teams in the true sense of minor league baseball. There's something called the A League in soccer, which is equivalent to Triple A in baseball or the CBA in basketball. There are players that come out of that every year. They don't exactly get "called up" because there's not a direct affiliation, but we're always looking there for good players, players who could help our team.

We scout through a number of different resources, through national team programs. Depending on the type of player we're looking for, there is a network of scouts and agents that we use. We do a lot of researching through videotapes, the Internet, and watching games on TV. The key to identifying a player is that it's not just a player – it's almost a salary amount that you would have to spend on that player. So, again, it goes back to a salary-cap management issue as much as player identification from a talent standpoint. We use the college draft to find young, usually American, players. Those who are coming out of college or young players in our youth national teams – under-17, under-18 – who have decided they wanted to play professional soccer, they go through the draft. The draft is usually for young players who won't dramatically make an impact on your team, but who you hope will help a little bit in their first year and, as they get more experience, will really be able to help more in the future.

Our oldest player is 30; our youngest player is 21. There are teams with 17- and 18-year-olds. Right now we haven't put a low-end limit on it. These young players are very special players, though; they can play and have incredible potential. Staying in high school or college, for them, isn't going to make their soccer skills any better, so it makes sense for them to move on if they're going to pursue a career in professional soccer. Size is important, but it's not a determining factor in whether you will be a successful soccer player or not. We have a player who is considered to be the next playmaker for our national team in Kyle Martino, and he's 5' 8", 145 pounds. Does he get knocked around? Absolutely, but you learn how to deal with that. I think that's part of what can make this sport great for a young person; you learn how to deal with the adversity of getting knocked around pretty good on the field while playing professionally. I'd be more concerned with the emotional and mental issues of a 16-, 17-, or 18-year-old than the physical issues, because it's a grind. Many people think professional athletes have it easy; they go to work for a couple of hours a day. It's a different mentality, a different grind, to be at the highest level of your sport. Imagine doing that at such a young age.

There's a process in our league to discover players from around the world who fall within certain salary parameters. That is done through our coaches and our "friends" – not technically scouts employed by our team, but player representatives around the world who everyone develops contacts with. Many times we'll go to one of those friends/scouts and say, "We need a left-sided defender," and we'll get a list of available left-sided defenders in our salary that we can look at and evaluate. Ideally we try to evaluate them in a live game situation or a live training by bringing them here to Columbus. Or, our coach will go watch them play in a game for their current club. Then, through the league, we work to acquire that player if we think he can help us. The league does our direct negotiation with the player's club, so the league acts as our legal representative to acquire the rights of the player for us.

Losing players to another league is a double-edged sword. There's a situation now in which Tim Howard, who was the best goalkeeper in this league, has been acquired by Manchester United. That's bad in the short term, but great for American soccer in that one of our players has gone to one of the most prestigious soccer organizations in the world and that they think that highly of this player coming from America. So it's part of the growing pains. As our sport continues to evolve, we certainly hope that we're going to continue to develop more players, but that from a business standpoint we'll have the revenues to acquire players of that caliber from other countries. I think we control the trend; we don't have to sell those players. When we talk about selling players, we're talking about transferring their rights and then we get a fee for that transfer. We control that business decision; the team and the league combined control the decision as to whether we're going to outright transfer a player to another league and take the money from that. We do a cost/benefit analysis on that transfer as anybody would in making any business decision. Is it worth the money we're going to get in losing this player, and what are the repercussions to the team and the league versus the amount of money we're going to get from it? You're valuing the asset –

the player, in this case – like you would if you were selling any other asset in business. From the player standpoint, we're no different from a Fortune 500 company; the only difference is that valuing our assets is a little more subjective than what a book value would tell you a building is worth.

In negotiations with players I'm pretty direct. There is always room for negotiation, but my starting point isn't that far off from where we're going to end up. I go in with a game plan in my mind of what's going to need to be done in dealing with the player's agent. I think everyone knows that there's a little bit of negotiation going on, but not big swings. Our mantra is open and honest. We'll tell the players where they stand and then we'll tell the agents, "This is what it's going to be if that player is going to be here in Columbus." We also reward for great performance, so it's not always a negative battle. Believe it or not, professional athletes in soccer take pay cuts to stay where they want to be or because they had a bad year. Find me one baseball player who's had a bad year who took a pay cut; there aren't many. That may be the most unique part of my job. Soccer GMs are the only ones who every year have professional athletes taking pay cuts because our salary cap doesn't go up high enough to reward players that had good years while keeping the guys that had bad years at the same salaries. Some agents are very good at convincing us their player had a good year. Actually, all agents are very good at fighting for their clients. You have say, "OK, stop fighting for your client. Let's switch chairs here and give me the straight-faced answer now. Your guy played in eight games this year; how can you expect a big increase?"

Looking to the Future

We need expansion. We need more teams in more markets. The MLS made a very smart business decision to contract the two teams in Florida.

From a sports team perspective, other than the Tampa Bay Buccaneers, there's not a lot of success in Florida. The league is moving forward with expansion wisely and cautiously by finding good investors who will support the single entity structure and who also have stadium plans. You've got to play in the right venue where you control your ancillaries in order to really make this successful.

I see our organization as a model soccer organization that will be recognized for its on- and off-field achievements. We always want to be a perennial championship contender while advancing the sport of soccer at the youth, club, collegiate, professional, and national team levels. So, what we believe here in our organization is that our short-term goal is always to win a championship and our long-term goal is always to grow the sport at all levels. That means being a partner in youth soccer, high school soccer, college soccer, club soccer, and the national team. That's why I think we're the most holistic soccer organization in this country; because we have a team of professionals who are dedicated to doing those things.

Jim Smith, the reigning MLS Executive of the Year, is in his third season as The Crew's General Manager. Smith was named the second GM in club history on Jan. 25, 2000, joining the organization after a successful four-year stint in the Athletic Department at Ohio State University. Smith oversaw tremendous growth and progress over the course of an eventful 2001 season - his second with The Crew - that featured an early-season coaching change and marked improvements both on the field and at the gate.

Following a 1-3-2 start, Smith had the unenviable task of replacing longtime head coach Tom Fitzgerald with then-assistant coach Greg Andrulis and the club went 12-4-4 the rest of the way, playing itself into the No. 4 seed in the 2001 MLS Cup Playoffs. Along the way, The Crew established a new club-record unbeaten streak of nine games (7-0-2) between July 4 and Aug. 19 and matched its all-time high point total (45) in six fewer games (26) than ever before. Off the field, The Crew's average attendance improved by 13.3 percent per game, from 15,451 in 2000 to 17,511 in 2001. Without the benefit of a fireworks-aided Fourth of July crowd or any doubleheaders, Columbus finished third in the league in attendance.

Smith was also instrumental in overseeing the administration of three of the most prestigious American soccer events of 2001 - the U.S.-Mexico World Cup qualifying match on Feb. 28, MLS Cup 2001 on Oct. 21 and the 2001 NCAA Men's College Cup on Dec. 14 and 16. Following the season, Smith was honored by his peers with the 2001 MLS Executive of the Year award.

Smith joined OSU in January of 1996 as Director of Marketing and Promotions before being promoted to Associate Athletic Director for Marketing and Communications in March of 1998. Prior to arriving at OSU, Smith was the Director of Live Event Marketing for the World Wrestling Federation from November 1994 to December 1995. He also worked as the Coliseum Director at Sam Houston State University in Huntsville, Texas, from May 1991 to November 1994. The Milford, Conn. native earned a Bachelor of Science degree in Radio, TV, and Film at Northwestern University and a Master of Arts in Sports Management at Ohio State.

Inside and Outside: Corporate America vs. the Sports Industry

Charley Armey
General Manager
St. Louis Rams

The Business

Sports business is unique because it's a combination of corporate America and entertainment America. You have a corporate atmosphere on the business side of the sports world, but you also have the entertainment aspect. That's basically what we're all about, in all the major sports. Even in the individual sports like tennis, you're still in the entertainment business, entertaining spectators. Sports is a delicate balance between the corporate world and the entertainment world.

The business side of the sports world is driven by the success of the sports team involved, unfortunately. If you're in the corporate world and have a good product, like Microsoft, you have a corner on the market and can generate your business with sales. In sports, the product that you put on the field or the court or wherever is what drives the business. The success of the business side is directly related to the individual success you have on the field of play; that's probably the biggest difference. It's considerably more difficult when you start talking about market share and things like this that are driven by the visible success your individual sports teams have.

For example, the biggest difference in my game, football, is the length of the season – not in terms of months or weeks, but in terms of number of games. Football has a short window of opportunity, with 16 regular season games, unlike hockey, baseball, or basketball. Your margin for success is a lot smaller in football than it is in any other sport. Your level of excellence has to be a lot higher because the stakes are higher in every game. In other words, the timeframe is the same in all sports – players work year-round to maintain excellence – but the exposure of the product to the community is much narrower, more fine-tuned, in football than in other sports. In contrast, when a player gets up to bat in the first inning of a baseball game and strikes out, he knows he'll probably have three more chances for success in that game. You don't strike out very often in football before you lose your opportunities.

The performance of a team has a huge impact on the business. When a team is winning, you can't get a ticket for a ballgame, but when they're losing, you can't give a ticket away. Once, when my team was down, I put four tickets on the windshield of my car for anyone who wanted to use them, and when I came back, there were eight. Business is generated by success.

Exposure

The major difference between running the business side of a sports team and running a big business is probably the exposure. If I'm running General Motors, for example, I have a large group of people working for me, but most people, outside of the general managers of my Fortune 500 club, don't see exactly what's going on in the inner workings. Outsiders know the top-level executives and the bottom line; they know GM is striving for market share. But they don't see all the things that get them to market share. The sports business is all visible. People see and feel results. Inside that Fortune 500 club, you can go along for years, keeping things that are happening from the public view, but you can't do that in sports. The exposure is probably the biggest difference.

People are more interested, believe it or not, in how well their hockey team, football team, basketball team, or baseball team is doing than they are in how productive the GM plant is in their city.

Sports has always been a release for people from anxieties and tensions – a source of relaxation. You don't get that in the business world. How many people know about the big tournament that GM put on for their employees last week? Very few, outside the employees. But if they selected baseball teams to have a tournament, everyone would know about it. The exposure factor is important because the entertainment side is just as important as the business side.

Perception, Image, and Community

As general manager, I have to be extremely conscious of how people perceive the whole St. Louis Rams organization. The people in our organization have to understand that we are a fan-based organization. People are interested in what's happening within the structure of our organization, from top to bottom.

You can go through any city in America, turn on an AM radio station, and listen to a sports talk show. More than any other single entity, ESPN probably brought this to focus in the last ten to 15 years because they are always keeping sports on the forefront. We have to be extremely conscious of the image of our organization, as well as the image of our football team. We have to maintain the image that we're a part of the community – and it's an accurate image, not a false one. We want to be part of the community, and we want the community to feel our involvement is a two-way street.

Roles, Structure, and Relationships

The Rams are unique in the way we're structured and in that we have probably one of the top people in the league in John Shaw, president of our organization, directly reporting to our ownership. He runs the organization more like corporate America, very hands-on. But he's also an excellent manager and lets his people do their various jobs.

We're very structured. We have our head coach, Mike Martz, and Jay Zygmunt, who is president of the football operation, overseeing all aspects of the football program, like football fields and football signings.

As general manager, the main thing I do with the organization is find players and make sure we try to stay on top of them. We have to know where the best players are, the players on other teams, and who has become a free agent. GMs are basically in the personnel business, trying to find the best possible players for your situation, for your chemistry, your ball club, who fit the philosophy and the personality of your head coach, and organization. It's a job that requires constant fine-tuning and attention.

My job is a continuous process. For example, I'm always reading our results and those of the players in the league and what we call the veteran players. I am continuously tracking them to see where they are going in their careers: Are they going up? Have they plateaued? Are they going down? I also have to keep track of injuries.

Preparing the draft every year is a huge job, a year-round job. For example, we have a draft at the end of April, and by the middle of May I am in meetings for the next year's draft already. It's a constant process of evaluating talent in the league, evaluating the talent you can get into the league, and evaluating the talent that has failed out of the league to see if someone will resurface, like Rams quarterback Kurt Warner.

I am constantly evaluating personalities, constantly looking for someone who can upgrade the position. There's an adage in sports that there's always somebody better at the position than the one you have. That's what is unique about sports: There's always somebody who can come along and knock out Joe Lewis, and you're always looking for that guy.

We evaluate everything, including Arena League and the Canadian Football League, from which we got a player last year, for example. We try to evaluate everybody who is active in our sport, in any league. There are a lot of Arena teams around, and we try to evaluate them and maintain relationships with them. Some of our teams even own some Arena teams. The Dallas Cowboys own two or three of the Arena League teams and use them as a minor league system, like baseball, to try to train and develop some of their players.

Players come from anywhere you can find them. We track all players and know their potential. Also, the chemistry and the opportunity have to be right. You have to balance many factors, as in corporate America, where you may find somebody who's very good in the computer part of the industry, but not very good at people management. You have to find the chemistry and the right balance and you are constantly looking to upgrade every position on your team. This vigilance is what generates and maintains our desired level of excellence.

What is unique about the Rams is the relationships we have with upper management and all the way down through the organization. We have a real, solid family atmosphere, and everybody functions well in his or her job. In almost any organization involving people, you'll have jealousies and cliques in the office, but we don't have that situation here.

In the Rams organization, everybody understands his or her role and tries to function within it, which makes everyone else's role function more smoothly. There is a strong overlap from personnel to Jay Zigmond, the president of the football operation, and a strong overlap in evaluating the players we are going to sign. The relationships have to be smooth – and they are. That we all get along so well, top to bottom, is largely attributable to the style of John Shaw, president of the Rams organization. He creates that atmosphere, where everyone seems to fit well and function well.

Goals, Visions, Objectives

Ultimately the goal for any sports team is to win the final championship. When we lost the Super Bowl in 2002, it felt as though everybody looked at us like losers. We set all kinds of records and had an unbelievable year; yet we were perceived as the losers.

In any sport, you are always trying to be better than your last performance. People remember the last game you played more than any game before that. So if you have to lose, lose early, not late.

In our business, we're perceived by what we are at any given point. We are always trying to strive for excellence, but there are so many variables that affect team sports. It is easier to have standards in individual sports. If you break a leg, you can't play tennis, and that's easy for everybody to understand. But if your team takes two or three injuries, you still have nine or ten people who can play, so everyone expects the level of performance to be the same. They don't realize the impact of losing key players.

Our organizational vision for the Rams is to continue to grow our fan base. We do that by continuing to improve our product from within. We don't limit our efforts to just the players on the football field; we include the front office, our sales people, our management team, the image of our ownership, and how we are perceived in our community.

Meet Us in St. Louis

Moving teams from city to city is ongoing. I wonder how many people know that in the early days of pro football, one of the best teams was the Providence, Rhode Island, Steam Rollers. Teams move for various reasons, including to improve their fan base and to change the image of the football team. There are many different reasons. A city that loses a team feels the economic impact of the loss, and the city that gains that team feels an impact in a positive way.

How we are perceived in the community within which we function, St. Louis, and how we are perceived within the community of the industry are both very important. We're trying to improve on our image with the high school coaches in our community, as well as the college coaches. Our success depends on the product we put on the field and the image we convey.

St. Louis is truly a sports-driven community. Some communities like particular sports, but St. Louis loves them all. If you present this community with a product that people can have pride in, it will not be difficult to get and maintain their interest. It's one of the greatest sports towns. They support their teams, and they like their sports, and they react to the functioning of the sports. The fan base doesn't give up on their team when they are having a hard time.

When we brought the team from Los Angeles to St. Louis, what helped with the move was the approach John Shaw took. He built an image for the team that fit into the Midwest. We had great support from people in the community that made it easy for us to adopt the personality of the area. Instead of getting our St. Louis fans to adapt to our California personality, we came in with the attitude that we needed to adopt the personality of the Midwest. That approach has been very successful for us.

Assigning Value

The number one factor for any team is its performance on the football field. It is the most visual and has the most impact. It is what national and local writers see and feel and communicate.

The second most important factor is the image you create off the field, with the players and within the organization. You have to fit into the community you're with, and that's been one of the great successes for Major League Baseball's Cardinals in St. Louis. They fit into the community, and the community feels the Cardinals are part of them – the same feeling they have with the Rams.

Achieving that atmosphere and that pride base is very important in any organization. We're not a closed environment, like corporate America. We're wide open, and everybody can visualize and fantasize what we are and what they would like us to be. That's how you are driven and how you become successful. If you continue to grow on that image, you'll continue to grow your fan base.

Winning championships is probably the number one factor in that kind of success, but not far behind is the image the players have within the pride-driven fan base of St. Louis. I like to think that the Aeneas Williams are part of the community. Having the players feel that they are part of the community is really important for building your fan base.

How to put a value on individual players is a very difficult question. A few of us will sit down and start assessing a player and his dollar value. The process is a complex monster. We have to maintain a discipline for determining how the player will function on the football field and how his performance correlates to wins and losses for us.

Other factors enter the assessment, too − the age factor, the player's medical history, how close he is to the end of his career. Some older players bring a unique chemistry because their presence may elevate the performance of younger players. It always boils down to how much he contributes both off the field and on the field. Most important is whether his presence will generate victories and lead to success for our football team. There is no formula − it's mostly a feeling, the proper instincts and the proper amount of experience. It's not easy to learn how to determine the value of players.

We have a huge payroll − a salary cap of 70-plus million dollars for an individual year. We have to meet those objectives. In that regard, football is no different from any business in corporate America. You want to show a profit margin at the end of the year, and there are many factors that go into trying to achieve that success. Many of our expenses, like any other business, are fixed expenses, and we know we will have certain kinds. You run into trouble in pro football when you have a salary cap and you go cash over cap, making it harder to meet your objectives.

When signing a player, we consider what he'll ultimately bring to the team and what he'll do for the franchise. Off the field, when we look for a scout, we look for how well he will fit into the chemistry of the organization. We work hard at trying to make sure we get the right people in our organization.

You have to have good television, radio, and ticket sales to generate revenue and run a football team with a profit margin. If a team has an idea that is unique and productive, there will be copycats just as in any other industry.

We try to maintain the level of excellence we think we have to have within the organization. The number one priority for us is product on the field. Nothing is harder on a sports franchise than major disappointment.

When your anticipation is high, a major disappointment is difficult. If there is a strong anticipation, you are expected to fulfill it year after year. We look at where we expect to be and try to achieve that goal.

Jay Zygmunt handles all of our negotiations. He has his own unique style. You handle veteran players completely differently from rookie players. You have a rookie salary cap you deal with, and you know pretty much what a third-round draft pick will make. Everybody knows those figures, but veteran players' salaries are based more on value. How much value does Marshall Faulk have with the St. Louis Rams?

We are the most fortunate team in the NFL to have John Shaw because he understands the longevity of the players and each player's value to the organization. The salary cap is difficult; there are many different factors to consider in making sure you can maintain a level of excellence and stay under the cap. It's not easy.

If you're running Ford Motor Company and you found an executive out there who could run the organization, you just do whatever you need to do to get him. It doesn't work that way in pro football because of the salary cap and other restrictions. If you go out to get player A because it will cost x dollars, it may cost you to lose player B, who is equally important to your football team. It's a delicate balance that's important to your success.

Recently I had a meeting with an executive of a major corporation. Within his organization are different divisions, and they hardly ever socialize with one another. They guard their individual territory, which makes it more difficult for the company to reach a common goal. We are fortunate to be able to avoid having that problem.

Losing a Super Bowl

Our anticipation was that all year we knew we had a good team and a highly functional team. As the season went on, we kept setting fantastic records on offense. Our fan base, our organization, the players, and our ownership all felt we would win the Super Bowl. Losing is a huge letdown when you have so much anticipation. If you're on a diet to lose 50 pounds and lose only 30, you are disappointed even though losing 30 was a big accomplishment. You have to be realistic that you can reach the goals you set for yourself.

Losing was difficult, but in St. Louis we have a strong fan base. It was even harder to feel successful from the business perspective because we had a disappointing year following the Super Bowl loss.

Now our success rides on how well we regroup and what kind of product we put on the field this year. For any business, not making an objective will have an adverse effect on the organization. Corporate America has its goals set, and if they don't succeed, it's a major disappointment for any organization. Our problems are not unlike those of corporate America – just more visible, everybody has a perception.

Public Eye

How we are perceived by the public is extremely important to the organization. That perception doesn't include only how well we play on the football field, but also how involved our players and organization are in community activities.

Bob Wallace oversees how we are perceived in the community and how well we interact with it. He does an outstanding job. John Shaw put him in that position to make sure this is a smooth and productive area of our organization. Whether we like it or not, if we're a sports team, how we are perceived by the public has a major effect on how well we'll succeed. That's the bottom line. We've all heard that if a player is good, people will tend to overlook some shortcomings, but at some point they become a factor.

All athletes have unique personalities, but all of them are ego-driven. If you have a whole herd of thoroughbreds, which are high-strung by nature, you work at that level all the time. Athletes are highly competitive, type-A personalities on all levels, and you have to try to manage these personalities. How well will a player handle knowing that he has to have knee surgery? Will he recover psychologically, as well as physically? Sometimes they don't. Sometimes an exceptionally good player has anticipated a great career in pro sports, but he gets an injury and, psychologically, never recovers from that injury.

Players are all Type As, all highly competitive, and all ego-driven, making sports management difficult, but most interesting. If you drove down the street today and got a speeding ticket going 110 miles per hour, you would go to a judge and pay the fine, and no one else would care. But if Kurt Warner got caught doing the same thing, everybody in America would know. Players have to learn to deal with the visibility of being a professional athlete, and the organization has to learn, as well.

What it Takes to be Successful

Ownership has to be solid, and the owner has to be willing to commit to have a successful franchise. If you don't have that, your job will be very difficult, and your level of performance will be low. It starts at that point and filters down through management, just as in any other company.

If you have a good manager, you'll probably make money; if you have a bad manager, you'll probably lose money. You can't get there if you don't have the proper ownership and commit to a level of excellence. We are lucky to have that here. Our chemistry is very good. People who jump into sports ownership from corporate America don't realize the huge difference in how they're perceived because they're now perceived from the outside, not from the inside.

I've been with a lot of pro football teams, and I was a college coach, but probably the best advice I've heard came from John Shaw. He talks about how you manage people and put them in position. He says it is the most important thing you'll do – managing the people in the whole organization, not just players. They're all unique, and all will require different management approaches.

Everybody should be working toward a common goal. If you have a 12-dog sled with a lead dog going in the right direction, everybody else will follow. If not, you won't get there.

People who want to work with us should know we're a glamour industry, but what we do is not glamorous – it's hard work. To get where we are is extremely difficult and requires a lot of time and energy. You must be willing to pay the price and commit to that sacrifice to be successful in the sports industry. A lot more goes into putting a football team on the field than just putting a uniform on and running them out there.

An NFL veteran of nearly a quarter century, Armey, oversees the Rams' college and pro personnel departments, among other responsibilities. Army, who joined the Rams following the 1997 NFL Draft, had spent the previous seven seasons (1991-97) with the New England Patriots as Assistant Director of Player Operations, negotiating with and signing drafted players and free agents. He also held the title of Director of College Scouting with New England.

Armey was a scout for the Atlanta Falcons from 1988-90 and a scout for the Green Bay Packers from 1985-87. He served the Denver Gold, Memphis Showboats, and Chicago Blitz of the USFL as an assistant coach, director of scouting, and as assistant general manager from 1983-85. He was the Gold's head coach for one game in 1983 and was a scout for the Buffalo Bills from 1978-82.

Charley began his career as linebackers coach at North Dakota State in 1968, was head coach and athletic director at Montana Tech from 1969-70, defensive coordinator at Montana, 1971-73, and assistant head coach and offensive and defensive coordinator at Colorado State from 1973-78.

Armey, a four-year veteran of the U.S. Navy, holds a bachelor's degree from Valley City State in North Dakota and a master's degree from North Dakota State.

Building a Franchise for the Long Haul – Locally and Globally

Doug Hamilton
Vice President and General Manager
Los Angeles Galaxy – Major League Soccer

Running a professional sports team is no different than running any other multi-faceted business. It is a business that relies on a variety of factors to ensure its success. A good organization realizes its place within the sporting and business communities. The following chapter will highlight some the critical elements to running a successful sports team through the eyes of Doug Hamilton, Vice President/General Manager of the 2002 MLS Cup Champion Los Angeles Galaxy.

Integration into the Community

In order for any professional sports team to be fully accepted and integrated into the consciousness of the community it represents, it must make an effort to reach out to the marketplace and assume responsibility as a good corporate citizen.

There are many ways to establish this relationship. Team management must take an active role in leading the organization's push for community integration by coordinating events with corporate leaders and making them aware of the presence of the team.

Players, in addition to their work on the field, must also do their part in integrating the team into the community it represents. Whether it is through community appearances for a sponsor or other community activities, the goal is to have fans in the market associate and the team for which they play. In a sport like soccer, where such a tight knit community exists, teams must also make a concerted effort to target the various youth leagues in their respective markets.

Clubs in Major League Soccer need to try and establish relationships with all of the influential people in their local soccer community. In Southern California, they are the leaders of the Coast Soccer League, the California Youth Soccer Association, and the American Youth Soccer

Organization (AYSO), as well as the many unaffiliated ethnic leagues in the area. The Galaxy are trying to be a part of what is meaningful to those groups and trying to make them a part of the club.

Additionally, the Galaxy organization must make itself the premier soccer resource in Southern California. Players coming through the youth systems in the market need to know that the Galaxy is doing their share to aid in their development. Though it is impossible to affect each of the many youths playing the game individually, we have to set up programs that will be beneficial to them.

Working with the leagues to develop players that may one day have the opportunity to play for the Galaxy is just one such vehicle. In order for good players to come out of the aforementioned leagues, they need to have the proper coaching. Therefore, the franchise has made a concerted effort to host coaching clinics where the technical staff works directly with some of the youth soccer coaches to give them a feel for how the professional game is taught.

Because soccer is a business, the Galaxy strives to support the youth organizations through various marketing efforts. In comprehensive agreements the club recently formalized with AYSO, CSL and CYSA, all parties will benefit from each other's resources, expertise and members.

Keys to Financial Success

Professional sports is a business; a complex one at that. A good organization realizes its place within that business. In a market like Los Angeles where there were many teams in place before the Galaxy and MLS entered the fray, this is especially important.

After a team has understood both its and the league's position within a marketplace, the management must work strategically to fully integrate itself into the local business community. In order to come in and be successful, a viable business plan must be set up.

Another way to entrench the club in the consciousness of sports fans throughout the United States in local markets is by owning and operating our own soccer specific stadium. Los Angeles and Columbus have already taken this step, while Dallas has announced plans to do so in time for the 2005 season. This has meant a major boost in revenues for these teams, which will be discussed later in this chapter.

If MLS teams are not housed in a soccer specific stadium, being part of the organization which holds a primary stake in the stadium in which they play is important. The New England Revolution, for example, shares Gillette Stadium with the NFL's New England Patriots, who are both owned by Robert Kraft. Therefore, the soccer team is able to obtain a greater share in the revenues generated in the stadium during their games.

Who owns the teams in any league is also of the utmost importance. Each team in MLS is managed in a way that is consistent with the strategy of other properties of the owner. One can use the Galaxy's structure as an example.

AEG, who owns and operates the Galaxy, is a fairly influential corporate citizen here in Los Angeles. We operate The Home Depot Center, Staples Center, Kodak Theatre and a variety of other properties. As an organization, we have the opportunity to leverage our assets better than some other clubs around the league. The Galaxy tries to take advantage of that situation.

Within AEG's corporate structure, the Galaxy must decide what type of niche we want to carve out locally and nationally. The club is marketing to what many people consider "the new America" – people in the various ethnic communities that call the United States home and came into this country with a knowledge and passion for this sport. It's our job to turn their passion for the sport and their favorite clubs abroad into commitment and loyalty to the clubs here in the United States.

As General Manager of the Los Angeles Galaxy, my role is to set the tone and direction of the organization. The many different disciplines in the organization function effectively and collectively. This ensures that customers will hear a collective tone from us. It does not matter which of our departments is out in the community representing the club: ticket sales, marketing, communications, or corporate partnerships.

Attracting Fans

The key to building a fan base is giving fans exciting players and an inspirational setting in which to watch the game. At the end of the day, you need people for whom this is a lifestyle choice, people who are emotionally and financially committed to the club. They support soccer not because of results, maybe even despite of results at times. They are in it for the long term and have made an investment in the club. They are season ticket holders and multi-game pack holders, the people we see on a regular basis.

Increasing a club's fan base each year is key to long-term success. Driving attendance up is critical. Maintaining a blue-chip corporate partner list is also important. Reaching out and finding ways to drive people to the facility is significant.

Revenue streams are pretty straightforward in sport – we need to put more people through the gates, gain greater financial commitment from our corporate partners and put enough value behind our broadcast rights so that we can start charging rights fees. When those three things happen in soccer, the sport will be increasingly financially stabile.

Profitability: Controlling Revenue Streams

The biggest step toward turning a profit in MLS is the one the Galaxy took – owning and operating the facility in which our teams play. Having your own stadium to call home is the greatest single dial-mover in terms of revenue. Additionally, our share of revenue streams is proportionally higher than the teams in MLS who rent their facilities as secondary or even tertiary tenants.

One of the keys to a financially successful franchise, in this league or any other, is controlling revenue streams. It is of the utmost importance to invest in brick and mortar and to build a facility. Now that the club has moved into The Home Depot Center, the Galaxy has increased our revenues from parking, concessions, and merchandise; we are in a much better situation versus those who rent.

Once in your own facility, you can control the dates and times on which you play. When controlling playing dates, you can play your games at optimal times, when there is the greatest opportunity for success. Not only will gate revenues be higher, but broadcast rights and sponsorship revenue will be as well. Our new facility lends itself well to greater corporate partnership involvement, which in turn allows us to ask for greater financial commitment from our partners.

Having our own stadium is a tremendous advantage. When ownership makes the statement AEG made, investing $200 million in a facility built for a club, it tells those who play for us and those in our fan base that we're here to stay.

The building of The Home Depot Center is the largest investment in brick and mortar that our sport has ever seen in the United States. The building itself gives people a great deal of comfort that we are going to be here for a long time. That is important for our fans to know. They have seen our sport come and go in cities before, and they've seen teams in Los Angeles come and go, too. For them to know we're no longer somebody else's tenant gives us great credibility among our fan base, players and employees.

The long-term viability of any franchise or any league is controlling revenue streams. Whether it's in Columbus Crew Stadium or the Home Depot Center here in Los Angeles, or the new facility that will be built in Dallas, MLS teams are getting a bigger piece of the financial pie.

Team and Front Office Personnel

It's important for the Galaxy to represent the community in which we work and live. That does not mean necessarily having a player on our roster from the major ethnic groups in our community, but it does mean putting a vibrant, exciting, ethnically diverse product on the field to represent Los Angeles. It is also important to have local kids who have grown up and succeeded in Southern California on the roster.

In our front office staff, we're looking for solid business acumen. Everyone employed by the team must have a sense of the market as a whole and understand how he/she can help the team succeed in that market. Whether it is a ticket sales person or a marketing person, knowledge of how to integrate the club's vision into the community is necessary.

Success in Major League Soccer is often driven by results, especially for general managers and the technical staff. These individuals are often judged by the performance of others. Coaches and general managers are hired only to later be fired at some point. Much like the sporting world, in corporate America, the days when a kid gets a job out of college, stays for 35 years, and retires with the same company are gone.

There has to be an environment where people can be successful, and that goes for both on and off the field. You have to allow people the freedom to make decisions. You have to give them the resources to get the job done and the space in which to do it. Our people need to understand the broad parameters in which we work and the direction we're taking. They need to be able to communicate the vision of the club and to make business decisions based on that vision.

An organization must recruit, train, hire and retain good people. They must be given the resources to do the job for which they are hired. Their vision for the club must be in line with the stated vision.

Does working within a salary budget keep teams on level ground? Records suggest otherwise. It merely keeps teams on an even spend. Is the model we see in baseball or hockey particularly successful at this point? The NBA has a luxury tax that lets them go over the cap. In our league, we play within that budget.

The challenge and responsibility is to find players who allow a team to be as entertaining and as successful as possible within that budget. There are considerable bargains, and there are great players, but if they are wildly successful and you have pay them more than you can afford under the budget, then you have to find the next one.

Special Events and Assuming the Risks

As a team in Major League Soccer, the Galaxy has the chance to be involved in hosting any number of types of non-league events. Whether it is a match in the Lamar Hunt U.S. Open Cup in which we play, an international friendly match involving our team, or a match involving two non-MLS teams, we are always open to bringing more soccer to The Home Depot Center.

A friendly match between a team from abroad and a MLS team can accomplish a number of objectives. Sometimes it gives a little something back to those people who are emotionally and financially committed to the sport in a different part of the world.

An additional purpose is marketing – to introduce our product. If they are not committed to an MLS club, it gets them in the building to see our level of play and convinces them that we're worthy of their support.

Sometimes we put on those games because a particular market wants that game. This gets back to what was mentioned earlier – the Galaxy needs to become a resource for soccer in our community. Sometimes a community like Los Angeles wants to see a Mexican team play against a team from Central America. If that game is taking place in our market anyway, the Galaxy should be a part of it. The club should have an influence on when and how that game is presented.

We measure the risk of putting on a special event based on a couple of factors. One is *Return on Investment (ROI)*. Secondly, some sort of tangible or intangible number we put against it in terms of marketing value, either to a particular corporate partner we have or to our ability to market to people who love our sport already but might not love us – yet.

Then we make the decision. If the event fits our calendar, if it fits our needs, if we think it will be a resource for the community, maybe we will do it after considering the toll it would take on our players. With the league schedule, the U.S. Open Cup schedule, and the international matches we play, the calendar gets crowded quickly.

MLS's Impact on the Global Soccer Scene

MLS becoming a World Class league depends on several factors. Most important is the quality of the product on the field. We have proven we can attract players and develop players who have significant impact on a global stage. If you look at the results of the U.S. National Team in the 2002 FIFA World Cup and consider that half that team was made up of MLS players, that bodes well for us.

Our ability to attract players like Guatemalan International Carlos Ruiz, who has an incredibly bright future, and Hong Myung Bo, who has played in four World Cups and was awarded the Adidas Bronze Ball in Korea, to come here and play in our league speaks volumes about our level of play and the respect this league receives around the world.

We need to continue to better market our product. We must attract those people who are emotionally and financially committed to this sport to be committed to the Galaxy and MLS. We need to increase our presence in the general media. Those things all take time. We are improving and will continue to improve. There are things we could do better, but we are well on our way to being a league that is respected around the world. Just last year, only four or five leagues in the world had an average attendance better than ours. We have made enormous strides.

Our investors in the league are committed for the long term and bring to the table a great deal of business acumen and success, demonstrated time and time again. As we announce each new facility going up, it tells people we have developed a business model we think makes sense, and that we're willing to put considerable resources behind the development of the facilities.

The sport has changed dramatically. For 40 years our sport was limited to teams that rented their facilities from owners in other sports. Now, thanks to Columbus and Los Angeles, we have moved into our buildings and let people know we are financially viable, drawing national and global attention to our league.

Examples of the bright future we are constructing are endless. Expansion in MLS is coming sooner than later. MLS will become more of a player on the global pitch. You will see other leagues follow our model of single entity and greater cooperation on the player development side between professional and amateur ranks. And I think you'll see broadcast rights and broadcast presence on a national level increase significantly.

Look at the direction of the league, which is solid. Ownership is investing in facilities, and that trend needs to continue. We need to continue to have more and more decisions driven at the club level, and more ownership and responsibility placed on the club to manage broadcast and other aspects of our league. There isn't a lot I would change, knowing that we're just eight years in and that we have ownership committed for the long haul.

To maintain the upswing of success, MLS must continue to place a value on its product. A vision must be communicated to those emotionally and financially committed to the sport and make them emotionally and financially committed to the league and the individual club. That will determine the level of immediate and long-term success attained.

Advice for those entering sports management:

"When evaluating market trends, we should consider that it is not what they say, it is also what they do."
-- Peter Moore, Sporting Goods and Equipment Industry Pioneer

Doug Hamilton was named the Los Angeles Galaxy's Vice President and General Manager on January 14, 2002. Hamilton oversees all aspects of the day-to-day operations of the Galaxy including the club's strategic marketing, public relations, corporate partnerships, community development, ticket operations and sales. Additionally, Hamilton will continue to oversee team and player personnel matters working closely with Head Coach Sigi Schmid.

Hamilton is leading the team's transition into The Home Depot Center - already considered perhaps the finest soccer stadium in the Americas. He is responsible for the design and implementation of new strategies to ensure that the 27,000 seats facility more than satisfies the expectations of soccer fans and team/venue sponsors participating in this historic facility launch.

Under Hamilton's leadership in 2002 team attendance increased by 10% to 19,047, finishing second-best in MLS. The organization stepped up its outreach with a significant number of targeted programs touching the soccer savvy Mexican, El Salvadoran, Guatemalan, Honduran and Korean communities in the ethnically diverse city of Los Angeles. The Galaxy also strengthened local ties with new innovative partnerships with AYSO and CYSA-S, and immensely improved service and communication with youth soccer teams and leagues throughout Southern California.

Not resting on the laurels of winning MLS Cup 2002, two weeks after the victory, Hamilton announced the acquisition of world class Korean defender Hong Myung Bo. Hong - the first Korean to play in MLS - captained the South Korean team to the 2002 FIFA World Cup semifinals, earning the Adidas Bronze Ball to finish as the third ranked player behind Ronaldo (Brazil) and Oliver Kahn (Germany) at the 2002 World Cup. In addition, he arranged to bring in Honduran international Alex Pineda Chacon - the 2001 MLS Honda Most Valuable Player and Budweiser Scoring Champion. In the 2001-2002 off season, Hamilton was instrumental in obtaining three outstanding acquisitions, which included Guatemalan International Carlos Ruiz, U.S. Olympian Chris Albright and Jamaican International Tyrone Marshall.

With a wealth of soccer experience as a player, coach and executive, Hamilton joined the Galaxy after serving as the Miami Fusion's Executive VP and General Manager from February 2000 to January 2002. Prior to the Fusion, Hamilton worked for six years for Adidas America, where he held the post of Director of Sports Marketing Latin America after successfully serving as Business Unit Manager of soccer and basketball. Hamilton is a graduate of the University of North Carolina at Greensboro with a B.A. in Physical Education.

The Three Components of the Sports Industry

Mike O'Connell
Vice President and General Manager
Boston Bruins

The Industry in Brief

There are three components to the sports industry: the entertainment component, the talent and competitive component, and the business component. In hockey, you have to try to put a team on the ice that the fans can be entertained watching, a team that will be competitive against the other teams in the league, and also a team that can be fiscally responsible. Each of these components is significant, though they are all intertwined. At certain times for the team, the business side has to be more in focus, at certain times the talent has to be more in focus, and at certain times the entertainment factor has to be more in focus. You have to make sure that the balance is there and appropriate at all times.

If your budget is too high, for instance, you have to try to reduce that in a way that does not affect the other two components. If you have the talent, you move it to help you in the future. If you are not an entertaining team, you look for an exciting player to make you more entertaining. At different times during the season, it's often appropriate to readjust the balance.

Our industry is different from most businesses because of the entertainment aspect of it. We are dealing with people who are involved with entertainment and have a professional skill that puts them in the spotlight so that they can become stars. We are dealing with athletes who are recognized on TV all of the time; they are recognized around the community. We are dealing with the press on a daily basis. You try to get them all to work together to create a positive image on the ice, in the dressing room, and through out the community.

Managing a Workforce of Athletes

Managing a workforce of athletes is a challenge. Having been an athlete, I know that it can be a very rewarding experience when you win, and when you lose, it's disheartening. But we have to find a way to get these players to play hard for each other. That's the job of the coach and the manager.

As GM, hiring the coach is my responsibility with input from senior management, scouts, and former players. The GM also acquires most of the players. The style of play, to some degree, comes from the GM office. Based on how you would like a team to win, you try to acquire certain types of players. But that really comes from the coach. You manage the coach, the coach manages the players, and during the season you handle the logistical work behind the scenes. You make sure it all works out.

The coach basically looks after the requirements of the players from day to day, which is a tremendous job. It is a tremendously difficult job to make sure that there's a believable game plan in place. The coach has to get every player to understand it and to execute it, and then to make sure that the conditioning level of the team is where it should be. He also makes sure that the motivation of the team is where it should be. That's a very difficult job to deal with in an 82-game schedule over 200 days. Motivating the team and keeping all the athletes sharp is very difficult to do.

Changing the coach is a lot easier than changing the players. We are constantly trying to find a match that works for the team. Personal issues can get in the way as well. You get a few injuries and all of a sudden the team is different and the coach has to coach in a different way. It's very difficult to balance it correctly, and be successful with 22 or 23 individuals per team, and know where to go and what's going on in their lives.

In the office, we try to hire only people who understand hockey, what hockey means to people here in Boston, and, more specifically, what the Bruins mean to the community. Those are the people that we look to hire. I am very parochial in who I hire here because of that fact. I want them to understand the fan's passion for the Bruins.

Hiring and Retaining Players

We have a minor league team down in Providence, which is our farm team. All of the players on the farm team are also signed through this office. Those players often include our young draft picks or draft picks from previous years. They usually play for a couple of seasons down in Providence before they are ready to come and play for the Bruins. Those are usually players that we get from the draft, or young players, or those we get through free agency. All of that comes through this department. I also have an assistant general manager who handles many of the scouting duties.

Hockey is a global game, so we have a director of European scouting who lives in Prague. He will see all of the young players over in Russia, Finland, Czech Republic, Slovakia, Sweden – wherever they may be. He has two or three scouts who work for him over there. In North America, we have scouts in the West and we have Canadian Junior League scouts in Ontario and scouts in Québec. We have three major scouts out there who cross over to make sure that they see all the players and they compare notes. We also have scouts here in Boston. These are all amateur scouts. We have a staff of three pro scouts who scout the pros only, to get scouting reports on players. If we want to make a trade with the New York Rangers, for example, we know their team, we've had scouts out to see their team, their amateur players, and their minor-league players. So if we want to make a trade, we can get it done with a pretty good understanding of what each team has. We use our pro scouts and amateur scouts who should have seen most of the players that another team has the rights to. They see them play the national league, and we see them play the minor leagues. So if there's a trade to be made between clubs, we can make the best-informed trade possible.

We usually start looking at players who are about 17 or 18. The draft age is 19, but usually when you watch a 19-year-old play, you also notice their team members, who are often 16 or 17-year-olds. You keep your eye on them, you make notes, and you watch them as they grow and mature. You identify them. Some of them mature into great players and some of them don't; some of them mature later. But it's good to keep a handle on them as well.

We feel that it is important to have locals, too. It's a terrific incentive to keep these kids playing. It gives them hope. So we try to recruit at least a couple from the Boston area every year.

Although you rarely see players stay with one team throughout their careers, especially in hockey, it can often be a benefit to retain older players. I feel that if a player is still an important member of the team on the ice, it helps to maintain continuity. Older players can help the new ones realize what was successful in the past. They have the ability to pass the torch, in a way.

The type of recruitment that you pursue often depends upon opportunities. As you assess your players and your teams at the end of the season, you look at what you need and what you don't need, where you might have an excess, and possible scenarios through which you can improve your team. You look at all of those factors. In a draft, you probably won't improve your team for about three years. You won't see those players really affect your team for three years. There are exceptions to the rule, of course. But you have to have a good solid base for these players to come to, if they are going to excel. They can't come to a team with all young players. You have to build it through many methods – through the draft, through trading.

Teams are often looking to get rid of players. For example, they might have too many left-wingers, or a player might have problems with the coach. Whatever the reason, every team has its issues.

When you look to move players in, you want to see if there's a match. You look at the value of the player. You look at the player's performance and compare that to what you're looking for. If the value of the player fits, you will acquire him.

Because of money issues, trades are much more difficult these days than they ever have been before. Players have to become available. If you're going to make a substantial trade, you're going to be getting a substantial player on your team. You have to have a match – the players have to equal their trades. It's often a difficult situation to find an even swap. Then you have to make sure that the player's salary matches up. The competitive issue has a way of affecting your team where you have needs. Every team is different; every team has needs, but each team's depth and financial state is different. So the trade route is difficult, but it can be done. We have done it successfully a number of times. It gets harder and harder each year, though.

You want the best athletes you can get. Character is a huge issue in team sports, however. Players have to be able to get along with each other and pull for each other. Players need to understand the necessity of teamwork, and there's also a courage component. Courage is a huge part of playing hockey. The player has to have the necessary courage to go where it hurts. He has to have the athleticism, the speed, and the agility as well. Clearly, the skill level is also very important in finding the right players.

It is part of my job to have my fingers on the pulse of the team. I have to know how the players feel, how the coaches feel, how the trainers feel, how the media feels, and how the fans feel. I have to try to make my decisions based on the performance of the team and their work ethic. When you make a coaching change or player change, you have to base your decision on all of those factors. If you let a big name go, there might be a reason for that – because he's costing you an exorbitant amount of money, for example. Or you may have a group of players that can't handle the coach, so the coach is out.

I do talk to the players, but I am more of a business associate. I am not in there every day, but if I see them, I'll ask about their day, or if I see something that needs to be corrected, I will definitely talk to players regarding their game. I really leave most of that up to the coaches, though. If there's a defenseman that I can help out because I was a defenseman, then I will talk to the coach first, to make sure we are consistent. Having been a former player, there's a credibility that comes with my general managing. There's an understanding that I've been through what they're going through, and that I do understand.

Making Money in Sports

The Bruins obtain the majority of revenues through television and ticket sales. We play in the FleetCenter for 41 days, and although the same company owns the Bruins and the FleetCenter, we get our share of the concessions when we are playing. We don't get a dime when the Celtics play, for example. There is also a component of product licensing that is shared by the NHL. We do get a percentage of Bruins jerseys that are sold, for example, but most of our revenue comes from tickets and media. We have sponsorships, but very few. There are some merchandise sales.

There are two issues that need to be addressed with regard to increasing profits: success on the ice and watching the player costs. Those are the two biggest concerns. Unfortunately, when your team does well, the players get more money. So you have to have some kind of system to replace the players when they become too expensive. Is it worthwhile to sign a huge name to get people in the door? It may work, but it depends on the success of the team. You could sign a huge player, but if you don't win, people will forget why you signed that player. So it depends on whether or not you win; it's a big gamble to take. So when we go to sign a player, we look at his ice time, his minutes, what he means to our team, how important he is, and then we go to the market. Based on all of those criteria, he will be weighed differently. For the players who have arbitration rights, we go right to the market. We tell the player, "This is where the market is pointing to, and this is what we will give you." If a player says that he wants X dollars, or two times that, then we tell them we can't pay it.

You're better off developing a system that allows you to keep replacing players; you have to have a steady stream of young players coming in that keep your team strong, and have five or six core players that are going to be there for a long time. Hopefully, when the time comes, you'll have developed a younger new core to replace them as well.

In order to increase revenues from year to year, you need to win more games. Tickets have to be desirable; people must want to see the Bruins. All of our games are on TV, and the FleetCenter can be a tricky place to get to. If you look at the construction in Boston, the construction on the Big Dig surrounds the FleetCenter. So in the last five years it has been a very difficult place to get to. When construction is completed, hopefully there will be a new collective bargaining agreement in place and the area will become a better environment for all to come see hockey in. If we can get the player costs in order, everyone should benefit, including the fans. Hockey tickets are very expensive. But it's also very difficult because of the player costs involved in running a team. We spend a higher percentage of our revenue on player costs than any other team in Boston, which is common for hockey teams. It's a bit out of line; if we had very high TV revenues, we could understand spending $40 million on payroll, but we don't. Payroll is by far the biggest expense that a team has. So it's very difficult. The biggest challenge in our sport is to make sure that it's profitable for everyone. It has to be a good experience for the fans, the players should get their share, and the owners shouldn't lose money.

The Bottom Line

The margins have become very thin. There's a fine line between making money and not making money. One player, a star player, could cost over $5 million, and that is the difference between making money and losing money. Sometimes it's even higher – star players can cost $9 million now, and that can cause serious problems.

In hockey there's an arbitration system. When you sign contracts for any player, you need to think about the player. Once you sign him, it affects you and everybody else. If there are two teams out West, for instance, that sign 10-goal scorers, and they pay them each $3 million, the Boston Bruins might have a 10-goal scorer who now has arbitration rights. There's a chance, then, of the Bruins having to pay him $3 million as well. In hockey, there are many reasons we may pay a certain player a little bit more. Maybe he fights for you. Maybe he's a crowd favorite. Maybe he's a very defensive player. On another team, the player may be very selfish – he scores 10 goals, but he might be selfish, a loner, or disruptive. So you end up with an independent arbitrator who has some knowledge of the game but does not know the inner workings of the team. What other teams do in the business affects everyone else.

Strong fans have a terrific effect on the bottom line. We want to make it so that the fans want to come. We're in the sports and entertainment business, after all. We want fans to come and enjoy themselves, and we want them to bring their children and have a great time. We play in a first-class facility; it's a terrific place to come. We make it very comfortable. Once you get here, it's an easy place to get around, and we want to make sure that we have a good product to sell. The games are enjoyable to watch.

A championship also has a fabulous effect on the bottom line – in any sport, not just hockey championships. But after such a season, it becomes very hard to keep winning because of the money that the players demand. You see it in every sport. The championship has an effect – it creates value for your franchise and for your brand. You try to keep it together and keep following it. You hope that the players' escalating salaries weigh into that potential profit. You can look at a number of cases. For example, the New Jersey Devils seem to be in the championship every year now, and they have done a fabulous job. They have an outstanding goaltender and an outstanding leader in Scott Stevens. They have built a team and have played the same way for 10 years, regardless of the coach. They have had successes. I don't know how much money they're making, but they've done a terrific job. The players that they have acquired, they eventually let go and bring in new ones. Their success is based on their sound defense system.

Achieving Success and Maintaining the Fan Base

I look at the three things in defining success. First, you have to be competitive on the ice; you have to give yourself a chance to compete for the Stanley Cup each year. Second, you have to be an entertaining team, a team that people want to come and watch. And third, you have to have a sound and structured business plan. Running a sports team is not very different from running any business, except that we have the entertainment aspect. We have a very public company – not in terms of ownership, but in the sense that it's part of the community.

We want to preserve the value of the franchise, continue to make the Bruins brand a desirable one to be associated with, and be a profitable team financially. If you win, the people will come. You have to have a chance to win, night in and night out. There are many variables that go into determining whether or not that happens, but you have to have the necessary depth – you have to have the necessary experience and youth to go into that formula – to give yourself a chance to win every night. If you do that, and the people have the expectation that the Bruins have a chance to win, it's going to be a great game. With a chance to win every night, the team is worth coming to watch. If you do win, it gives people more of a reason to come. And if you're entertaining on top of that, it's even better.

We make ourselves accessible; we try to make it as easy to get to us as possible. We have been here for a long time, so there is a built-in fan base. Going to the Bruins games is part of winter here in Boston. I became a fan of hockey by watching it on TV as a kid, going to the games, and playing it. The Bruins have a huge influence on kids; most of the kids who play hockey in Boston play because of watching the Bruins on TV. A lot of our fan base is made of people who have played hockey or people who play hockey now. It's a terrific game; a good hockey game is up and down – it's very exciting.

It is sometimes very difficult to maintain public appeal, though. People have criticized us here in Boston – especially the press – for not spending money, for letting players go. It's been difficult having to deal with the business side of it – having the information that we have and dealing with people who write or broadcast who don't have information with regard to revenues coming in. Again, the percentage of revenues we spend on players is greater than that of any other team in Boston. People don't want to hear that. It comes down to winning. We have to win games.

There's a certain dedication that emerges in a city, though. When a team is relocated, it's often a difficult situation. When a team moves, it's painful for the city they're leaving, but it's exciting for the players and for the city that they're going to play for; it's bittersweet. It also affects rivalries. Once Colorado moved from Québec to Colorado, their rivalries were instantly different. They became rivals of Detroit and St. Louis and the teams out there in the West. Rivalries are established a couple of ways: by familiarity and also by playing a team in the playoffs. Once you play a team in the playoffs, you develop a rivalry.

Sports Management Advice

To succeed in sports management, you have to do what you think is best. Pay attention to everyone around you, but ultimately you have to have the courage to make the decision. You have more information regarding the situation than does anyone else, so you have to make a decision and you cannot let public opinion get in your way. If you look at the three aspects of the business – the competitive issue, the financial issue, and the entertainment issue – you have to have a better handle on all three of those than anyone else. You have to make decisions based on what you know about the sport, the game, and your team.

Also, protect the value of the franchise. That's the only way you can ensure that the team will be around over the long term. If you lose money year after year, you lose your business.

Finally, run the business the way you run your life. Treat people like you want to be treated.

Mike O'Connell enters his fourth season as the team's General Manager, becoming just the sixth man in club history to hold that position when he was named to the post on November 1, 2000. He is also in his sixth season as the team's Vice President, and in these positions, he is involved in all aspects of the on-ice operation of the hockey club. Coming to his present post following six seasons as the club's Assistant General Manager, he has been instrumental in bringing much of the young talent into the organization and making key acquisitions to improve the club's performance, including the top record in the Eastern Conference and second overall in the league during the 2001-02 season.

O'Connell came to his current positions with over 20 years of experience as both a player and assistant coach in the National Hockey League and as a head coach in both the American and International Hockey Leagues. He turned professional with the Blackhawks organization in 1975 and played five-plus seasons with Chicago and their Central Hockey League affiliate in Dallas before coming to Boston on December 18, 1980 in a trade for Al Secord. He enjoyed his best NHL seasons during his six years in a Bruins uniform, recording 50+ point campaigns for three straight years from 1982-85 and representing the team in the 1984 NHL All-Star Game in New Jersey. He won the WSBK-TV 38 Seventh Player Award in 1983-84 and still holds the club record for consecutive games scoring a goal by a defenseman with a seven-game streak during that season. He was traded to Detroit for Reed Larson on March 10, 1986 and concluded his playing career with the Red Wings at the end of the 1989-90 season.

O'Connell then moved into the coaching ranks, assuming the head coaching position for the IHL's San Diego Gulls in 1990-91. As an independent team without the benefit of an NHL affiliation, he guided that club to a 30-45-8 record and then moved into the NHL, returning to Boston as an assistant coach. Working both behind the bench and from an evaluating position in the press box, he helped the club to a 36-32-12 record as they advanced to the Conference finals, despite losing over 500 man-games to injury.

On June 12, 1992, he was named as the head coach of Boston's American Hockey League affiliate in Providence. Working with many players who also wore a Boston uniform during his tenure, he compiled a 74-71-15 record over a two-year span and won a Northern Division title with the AHL Bruins in 1992-93. He then returned to Boston when he was named the club's Assistant General Manager on July 5, 1994.

Major League Soccer: Establishing the World's Sport in "A New America"

Don Garber
Commissioner
Major League Soccer

Sports leagues and their teams, like most businesses, deliver a product to a consumer and strive to be profitable for an owner or group of investors. To be successful, sports organizations require strong branding and effective marketing. With these strategies in place, fans will hear and read about their team every day and will care deeply about the players and team.

While many American consumers are very connected with countless household brands (Coke, Tide, M&M's, McDonald's, etc.), sports leagues, teams and players have a different and far more complicated relationship with their consumers, or "fans." It's a relationship that can last for many years, through wins and losses, player trades, name changes, and other forms of new branding.

Once the bond between a team and fan is forged, it can last for many years, and is often passed from one generation to the next. It thrives with victory and survives defeat. It's a relationship built on loyalty and trust, fueled by hope and excitement.

However, when the team/fan covenant is broken, it is nearly impossible to re-build the special and unique loyalty that exists between the two. Entire sports have suffered from not evolving their product to the changing needs of their fan base. Teams have lost fans who name their children after players, who plan their weddings and other family events around team schedules, and who live and die for their teams' success at each and every game.

It's All About the Fan

Sports teams and leagues succeed or fail by their relationship with the average fan. Rarely is there a consumer product that is as important to adults as it is to children; that spans widely diverse ethnic groups and is as important to the CEO in the corner office as it is to the employee on the factory floor. This "pan-demographic" quality requires decision making that is sensitive to the needs of a wide and diverse audience.

Team branding, player personnel decisions, marketing strategies, pricing policies, in-stadium operations and day-of-game logistics and entertainment must take into account their impact on every segment of the fan base.

This unique relationship is complicated by the belief among most fans that their local sports team exists "in the public domain," belonging to them just as much as it does to the team owner. The team, they believe, exists solely for their enjoyment.

Fans believe that profits and asset appreciation are far less important than winning games and league titles. Team owners believe they have the right to earn a profit with their sports investment. Their consumer/fan believes the team should win at any cost, with no regard for the "bottom line." This dichotomy creates a challenge unique to the sports business.

All Sports, All of the Time

Most products require extensive advertising and public relations budgets to build brand awareness and attract national and local exposure. The amount of media space and time devoted to sports rivals that provided to general news. Most significantly, this exposure comes virtually at no cost. Daily newspapers, television newscasts and radio talk shows each have dedicated reporters and space allocated to local and national sports news.

Beyond exposure in general media programs, an entire new sports media industry has emerged with both general and sports-specific news programs, talk shows, magazines and web sites.

The industry, from management to players, is expected to provide unprecedented access to reporters and columnists. While this access leads to massive free publicity, it also puts teams and players under enormous scrutiny and at times exposes the unpleasant side of the industry.

In addition to press coverage, most major league sports contests are televised on local, cable and network television and radio. These broadcasts, often lasting several hours in duration, are immensely valuable promotional vehicles for the team and the players, and in many cases, the sport itself.

Sell, Sell, Sell

College and Professional Sports represent a multi-billion dollar industry, competing against all other forms of entertainment for a share of consumer spending. With the proliferation of new leagues and teams – along with rising labor and operating costs – the generation and discovery of new revenue streams has become more important than ever before to ensure teams can be profitable and remain competitive on and off the playing field.

Revenue streams in sports come primarily from the sale of tickets, corporate sponsorship, fees from broadcasters, and stadium amenities (concessions, merchandise sales, signage, luxury boxes, and parking).

Competition exists not only among the major and minor leagues, but new sports are emerging on the scene which target new demographic groups and capture "niche" markets.

The demographic make-up of America has changed over the last generation. More young people are empowered to influence family decisions. Kids today are participating in new sports – from soccer to skateboarding – and will have a significant impact on their sports allegiances as they grow into important decision-makers. These emerging sports also provide inspirational elements for today's youth, as prior generations did not have the opportunity to envision themselves turning their passion into professional participation.

The so-called "Action" or "Extreme" sports (skateboarding, snowboarding, BMX biking, freestyle roller skating, etc.) provide young people the thrill of being a fan of a sport that they participate in at a greater frequency than the more established sports (football, baseball, basketball, and hockey).

Soccer 101

Though there are nearly 18 million soccer participants in the United States, MLS is challenged with converting those who play the game into being fans of the league, teams and players. MLS is clearly the new kid on the block. The League's advantage is that just as kids of a certain generation grew up with baseball, kids today are growing up on suburban soccer fields playing the game of soccer.

Grass Roots Soccer

First, soccer is the largest and fastest growing youth sport in America. Soccer participation is exploding at all levels, from the youngest "kinder-kickers" to the high school and college ranks. The ease of play for people of all ages, sizes and genders, combined with the minimal risk of physical injury, point to even greater levels of future participation. These legions of youth soccer players, and their families, affectionately called "soccer moms" and the "soccer mini-van generation" represent the future fans for Major League Soccer.

Additionally, immigrants from Latin and Central America represent the largest and fastest growing minority segment in America. Today, the U.S Hispanic population totals nearly 35 million people – primarily from Mexico and Central America – places where soccer is the dominant sport. This explosive immigration provides MLS with millions of potential fans that are not raised on the traditional American sports of football, baseball and basketball.

Lastly, it is no secret that soccer is the world's most popular sport. With little or no competition for fans or participants, soccer (or football as it is called outside the U.S.) dominates the sports market throughout Europe, Latin America and Asia. The internet and the expansion of cable and digital television now bring the world's most popular soccer teams in to millions of American homes.

Many popular international soccer clubs, from Manchester United (England), to FC Barcelona (Spain) and Chivas de Guadalajara (Mexico) have played actual live games in the United States.

Explosive Participation Growth

	1980	2001	% Change
Registered Youth	885,000	3,884,000	+339%
U.S. High Schools	190,000	625,000	+229%
NCAA Programs	600	1,500	+150%
NSCAA Registration (coaches)	2,300	16,000	+595%
Adult Registration	104,000 (1987)	250,000	+140%

The World Cup

The World Cup is the most popular sports event in the world, with more than 200 countries participating, millions of in-stadium fans and billions of television viewers world wide. The tournament began in 1930 in Uruguay and takes place every four years.

Different from other traditional American sports, each participating country establishes a National Team that competes in a variety of qualifying matches leading up to the World Cup. The players are "called-up" for national team duty from their respective professional teams. Many MLS players compete for their respective country's National Team, providing enormous exposure for the League and the sport on the world's largest stage.

This "dual duty" is both a great benefit to the League and a challenge. First, some of the League's best players leave their local team during the season and miss many days and weeks of League competition. However, when the U.S. National team is successful (as it was in 2002 when it reached the quarter-finals of the World Cup), the League can promote the fact that most of the players were from MLS rosters.

In 2002, MLS created a marketing campaign, "Strike Force: For Club and Country," featuring Landon Donovan, Brian McBride, DaMarcus Beasley and Clint Mathis – MLS players that performed brilliantly in the World Cup and became overnight stars upon returning home. American sports fans love success and reveled in the fact that for the first time, a men's U.S World Cup team succeeded on the international stage, soundly defeating powerful teams from Portugal and Mexico.

Professional Soccer in America

Soccer is the newest major professional sport in the United States. Leagues exist for both men and women. The first division league for men, Major League Soccer, was founded in 1996 and consists of ten teams playing from April through November. The Women's United Soccer Association, the first division league for women, was founded in 2001 and consists of eight teams playing from April through August.

Additionally, similar to other professional sports, soccer has its "minor" league – the United Soccer Leagues – consisting of a variety of development divisions from youth, amateur, semi-pro and professional.

Major League Soccer – The Early Years

Major League Soccer was formed immediately following the 1994 World Cup, one of the most popular sports events in world history. FIFA (Federacion International Football Association), the governing body for world soccer, granted the World Cup to the United States as a means to increase the popularity of the sport in this country. The United States Soccer Federation (U.S. Soccer), the national governing body for the sport, managed the World Cup and committed to start a Division I men's professional league as a World Cup legacy with profits generated from the event. Alan I. Rothenberg, the president of U.S. Soccer at the time, led the effort to form the league, and sought investors to own and operate teams throughout the country. Rothenberg was successful in attracting a blue-chip list of investors, including several experienced owners of teams in other major leagues, including Lamar Hunt (Kansas City Chiefs), Robert Kraft (New England Patriots) and Philip Anschutz (Los Angeles Kings). Additionally, several well-known business titans joined the group, including John Kluge (Metromedia), Ken Horowitz (Cellular One) – Horowitz didn't join until expansion in 1997 – George Soros (Soros Funds) and Dentsu (Japan's largest advertising agency).

The Investor/Operators provided $50 million in start-up funding to sign players. The League immediately hired staff, including its first commissioner, Douglas Logan, a former entertainment executive.

The Single Entity

Learning from some of the challenges and issues that other major sports league face as they have evolved, Rothenberg structured MLS as a limited-liability company with team owners investing in the league and operating local teams.

This "single-entity" structure was a groundbreaking development for professional sports. With the understanding that a fledgling soccer league faced enormous obstacles, not only from the other major leagues, but from international soccer clubs throughout the world, the founders planned to create a league where all the teams worked together to secure the long-term viability and success of professional soccer. The owners, or Investor/Operators, served as the MLS Board of Governors, and met regularly to establish long-range strategy.

The League paid the players and signed all player contracts, ensuring labor cost certainty. The first players were "allocated" to each team, and in subsequent years were drafted from the collegiate and youth soccer ranks.

The League sold and retained national revenues from broadcasting and sponsorship, and performed many game operation functions. Local teams controlled most local revenues, and paid a management fee to the League for the services it performed on their behalf in the form of a share of local ticket sales.

Upon the establishment of the MLS single entity structure, the National Football League Players Association (NFLPA) approached several MLS players who organized and brought legal action against the league claiming the structure was a violation of U.S. anti-trust law. The NFLPA feared that the MLS centralized structure would threaten economic opportunities for all players in professional sports. The lawsuit (Frasier, et al v. MLS) lasted from 1996 until 2000, when the trial was held in United States Federal Court, in Boston. After a three month trial, a jury found that the structure was legal.

The single-entity structure has since been adopted by most new sports leagues, including the WNBA, the National Lacrosse League and the Women's United Soccer Association.

The First Kick

MLS kicked out its first ball on April 6, 1996 when the San Jose Clash (now Earthquakes) met D.C. United at Spartan Stadium in front of a sold-out crowd.

Capitalizing on the interest and demand from the World Cup, the inaugural year was a huge success, with average attendance league-wide of over 17,000 fans.

A national broadcast agreement was formed with ABC Sports, ESPN and Spanish language broadcasters, Univision. Most MLS teams also forged relationships with local broadcast and radio stations. Considering that the NBA did not have its Championship Finals on network television until 1980, nearly 50 years after its founding, the MLS network, cable and local broadcast partnerships represented quite an accomplishment.

Major sponsorship agreements were signed with some of the biggest names in corporate America, including Pepsi-Cola, Honda, AT&T, Budweiser, FUJI Film and MasterCard. These sponsors not only paid fees for media on MLS broadcasts, but also utilized MLS players and trademarks in widespread promotional campaigns, providing the League with needed marketing exposure.

Most importantly, the league signed the top American soccer players that competed for the United States Men's National Soccer Team during the 1994 World Cup. American stars such as Tab Ramos, Tony Meola, John Harkes and Alexi Lalas joined MLS from Europe and Latin America, where many had signed professional contracts. MLS also signed many well-known international players. These players, from Mexico, Central America, and Europe, were strategically allocated to MLS cities where local ethnic fans could easily connect and identify with them.

Overall, the inaugural year was considered a huge success. Major League Soccer, though the newest professional sport in America, was quickly considered part of the domestic pro sports landscape, with local and national media coverage, a national broadcast agreement, major corporate sponsors, established owners and a growing fan base.

During the 1997 season, MLS capitalized on its successful launch, and expanded broadcast coverage on network television from three games on ABC Sports, to twelve. Several new major sponsors were added and media and consumer enthusiasm was high. However, the league suffered the "sophomore slump" at the gate and saw attendance decline nearly 20 percent.

In 1998, interest in the League remained high and MLS expanded by two cities, from ten to twelve teams. Important new markets were added in Miami and Chicago.

The 1998 World Cup took place in France. Four years after the successful 1994 World Cup in the U.S., the U.S Team performed poorly and finished last of the 32 teams that qualified to compete.

The 1998 and 1999 season saw continued decreases in attendance and television ratings. Prior to the end of the 1999 season, the MLS Board of Governors fired Doug Logan and brought in Don Garber, an executive with the National Football League as its new commissioner. Garber spent 16 years with the NFL in a variety of capacities, from marketing, corporate sponsorship sales, event production and as the head of NFL International, an organization responsible for the growth of the NFL brand overseas, particularly in Europe.

The theory was that if Garber could convince Europeans to love American football, he should be able to convince Americans to love soccer!

Major League Soccer Today

Major League Soccer has ten teams playing in cities throughout the United States.

Eastern Conference
NY/NY Metrostars
Chicago Fire
New England Revolution
D.C. United
Columbus Crew

Western Conference
Los Angeles Galaxy
Kansas City Wizards
San Jose Earthquakes
Dallas Burn
Colorado Rapids

The League for a New America

Launching a new professional sports league is a very difficult task in today's crowded sports marketplace. The four established major leagues in the United States (The NFL, NBA, MLB and NHL) have all been in operation for nearly one hundred years. Each has established their own unique position in American culture and history.

Baseball is "America's Pastime" – The World Series, Babe Ruth, Mickey Mantle, Hank Aaron, The Yankees, Cal Ripken, Mark McGuire and Sammy Sosa.

Football is tailgate parties – Monday Night Football, Jim Thorpe, Joe Namath, "The Steel Curtain," Joe Montana, Dan Marino

Hockey is The Stanley Cup -- the Montreal Canadiens, Bobby Hull, Wayne Gretzky

The NBA is "Showtime" – Michael Jordan, Shaq, The LA Lakers and New York Knicks.

Major League Soccer has yet to establish its "history," the memorable events that define its fabric and have become so much a part of the shared professional sports experience. However, the potential exists for professional soccer to capitalize on two major social and demographic trends in the United States to help MLS capture its piece of the valuable sports market.

It's Your Game

From a marketing perspective, the League's message is: "this is your game." *It is the game you love. It is the game you follow, whether you play, or follow a team from Barcelona or from Mexico. Now there is an MLS team right in your hometown, playing right here in your stadium in your community. Embrace it. Love it. Care for it. You now live in this country. You are participating in all of the great things that this country provides you with as an immigrant or as a resident. This is your team. Playing your game.*

Additionally, Major League Soccer and its teams dedicate significant resources to reach out and connect with the Hispanic community. The League has created a wide variety of Hispanic-targeted grass roots programs – from participatory soccer events, such as MLS Futbolito, to the Hispanic Heritage Nights at each stadium. Many MLS games are broadcast on Hispanic television and radio outlets and most MLS teams have Hispanic players.

Another effective marketing strategy utilized by MLS teams is to offer fans "double-header matches," where two international clubs will play in conjunction with an MLS game. This tactic helps to attract fans of these international teams, who may not yet be fans of MLS, with the hope that they appreciate and connect with the sport in their new homes.

The biggest opportunity for growth remains capturing the attention and participation of the millions of youth soccer players in the country. Though MLS is less than 10 years old, surveys have found that the League is the third "favorite" sport among kids ages 7-11 years old – a remarkable achievement for a young sport.

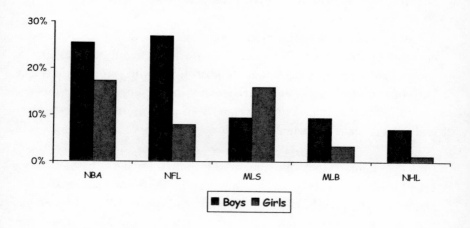

Soccer-Specific Stadiums

Every sport in America has a special home. Ebbets Field, Yankee Stadium, Fenway Park, Madison Square Garden, Wrigley Field, Soldier Field, and The Rose Bowl are all stadiums or arenas that have long, storied histories and a special place in the American sports scene.

Recently, sports teams have built new facilities that capture the unique relationship that fans have with their teams. Camden Yards harkens back to the familiar and cozy baseball stadiums of yesteryear. The Staples Center in Los Angeles provides the LA Lakers and LA Kings with a high tech theatre in the heart of Hollywood.

These new facilities not only represent the image and personality of the team, but also provide significant new revenue opportunities with luxury

123

boxes, club seating, and countless sponsorship of everything from the stadium itself, to signage throughout the facility

When Major League Soccer was founded, the league played games in large football stadiums. Teams were often secondary or tertiary tenants, with few opportunities to generate revenue beyond ticket sales.

It soon became obvious that soccer needed facilities that were appropriate for the sport; venues which offered a full size regulation soccer field, as opposed to smaller football fields with yard markings and hash marks; stadiums which were smaller in size and provided owners the opportunities to generate revenue from parking, merchandise sales, and other revenue opportunities.

In 1999, Lamar Hunt, the Investor/Operator of the Columbus Crew, established a new lexicon in American Sports – the soccer-specific stadium – when he built Crew Stadium in Columbus, Ohio. The stadium was sized appropriately for the team's average attendance (approximately 18,000 fans per game) with 23,000 seats, along with modest luxury boxes and other hospitality areas. It soon became a favorite facility for U.S. National Team matches and MLS special events. It also was utilized for high school sports events, concerts and other non-sports events.

In 2003, the Anschutz Entertainment Group opened the next generation of a soccer-specific stadium, The Home Depot Center. Considered the "cathedral" for soccer in the United States, The Home Depot Center evolved the concept for the Los Angeles market, and offered exclusive club seating, elaborate corporate suits, restaurants and large party rooms. The stadium has 27,000 seats, making it attractive to not only MLS games, but also international soccer matches and World Cup competition.

Players

Having a league where Americans can play year-round at home is so important for the development of soccer in this country. MLS has almost 200 young American players who are playing soccer in a professional environment day in and day out. This structured training and competition is raising the caliber of play and the quality of the American player.

Most of the best young soccer players in America play in Major League Soccer. Their salaries and benefits are the biggest expense item in the overall League financial plan.

Each MLS team has 18 senior players and several young developmental players. Teams are permitted to sign three international players, or foreign players who are not American citizens. Competition to sign these players comes from European and Latin American soccer teams that see the massive growth of the game in the U.S.

Expansion

Major League Soccer began with 10 teams, expanded to 12 teams in 1998 and then eliminated two teams in 2001. In the December, 2001, the MLS Board of Governors determined that by contracting the League by two teams – the Miami Fusion and Tampa Bay Mutiny – the League would be stronger and more financially viable. Both teams were struggling financially and had been unable to establish a strong fan base. By removing the financial burden of supporting these teams, the League could focus on building new stadiums, creating new marketing opportunities and importantly, finding new cities that expressed the interest and capability to support an MLS team.

MLS announced in 2002 that it would attempt to expand back to 12 teams for the 2005 season. The requirement for ownership is a committed ownership group, an appropriate soccer-specific stadium and a city that has a strong soccer community.

The Vision

Major League Soccer's vision is to be among the leading soccer leagues in the world and considered among the major sports leagues in America.

To achieve this goal, MLS has established a strategy to lead the sport of soccer on all levels – to be the "gateway" to the sport for fans, the media, participants and the international soccer community. MLS teams are very active in their local communities, though clinics, special events and many grass roots soccer programs.

The League office has established a new marketing company, Soccer United Marketing (SUM), to manage a wide variety of soccer programs, both on the grass roots and television level. SUM was established to exploit commercial soccer opportunities in areas that are both directly engaged in Major League Soccer and in those areas that are not involved with MLS. For example, SUM owns the English-language broadcast rights in the United States to the World Cup, as well as the Mexican National Soccer Team and other soccer properties.

The Challenge – The Opportunity

MLS faces enormous competition from the other major sports in the country and from the massive amount of entertainment and leisure options that exist for fans of all ages. Like any new business, establishing a strong brand, generating revenue and securing strong investors are all key priorities.

From a marketing perspective, MLS has the advantage of having a market of future fans built through the ever-growing numbers of soccer participants. However, converting soccer players into soccer fans takes both time and significant marketing resources. MLS teams have to convince people that they can extend their interest in the sport that they love so much as a player or that they share with their son or daughter as a soccer mom and dad. The best way to share that common soccer experience is to be a fan of their local team.

The future of professional soccer is less about "developing the market," and more about "converting the market." There are more than enough people who care about the game. To convert those who care into being fans requires getting them to attend and watch MLS games on television, grow their interest in MLS players and connect them closely with their local MLS team.

The market potential is enormous. Sports in America is a multi-billion dollar business, but more importantly, sports provides fans the opportunity to live in a world of dreams and fantasy. Successful teams and players should never forget that sports hold a special place in the hearts and minds of sports fans. For a few hours a week, they are part of something special and magical.

Since assuming Major League Soccer's top position in August of 1999, Don Garber's vision and commitment has enabled MLS to build a solid foundation for soccer in the United States and generate unprecedented momentum and progress for the sport. In 2002, Garber spearheaded the formation of the League's sister company, Soccer United Marketing (SUM), which purchased the English-language television rights for three

FIFA World Cup properties – Korea/Japan 2002, Women's World Cup China 2003 and Germany 2006. Under Garber's supervision, SUM packaged the FIFA rights with the League's five-year television deal on the Disney networks, ABC, ESPN and ESPN2 to provide the destination for televised soccer in the United States. At the helm of SUM, he also played an instrumental role in bringing the 2003 Women's World Cup to the U.S. after it was moved from the original host country, China, following the SARS outbreak.

Prior to becoming Commissioner of MLS, Garber was the senior vice president/managing director of NFL International, where he oversaw all aspects of the NFL outside the United States, including the NFL Europe League. Garber, who guided NFL International since its creation in 1996, managed a group that grew from five employees based in the NFL offices in New York, to a global organization of more than 130 people, with offices in six countries (Canada, Mexico, England, Germany and Japan). Revenues and profits increased significantly during his tenure.

Before being appointed as the head of NFL International, Garber was vice president of business development and special events for NFL Properties (NFLP), the marketing arm of the National Football League. This group, which he created in 1990, was responsible for all non-game NFL television programming and production, event marketing, grass roots activities and entertainment programming and was responsible for creating the sports event industry standard, the "NFL Experience."

Garber began his career at NFL Properties in 1984 as a marketing manager and became the League's Director of Marketing in 1988, with responsibilities for managing all national NFL corporate sponsorship sales and marketing. Garber is a member of the United States Soccer Federation Executive Committee, and also on the Board of Directors of the United States Soccer Foundation and the Soccer Hall of Fame Advisory Board. Outside of soccer, Garber is on the Advisory Board of the Hope & Hero's Pediatric Cancer Foundation at New York's Columbia Presbyterian Hospital; the Board of Directors of the National Campaign Against Youth Violence, a national anti-violence program, and the Board of Directors of Princeton Video Image, a high-tech broadcast company. He graduated with a degree in business and journalism from the State University of New York, College at Oneonta, where he was president of his senior class.

Building Success through Sports Management

Mike Smith

General Manager
Chicago Blackhawks

Basics of the Sports Business

The sports business is part of the larger entertainment industry. Some think sports is separate from the entertainment industry, or not as linked to it, but it is really part of the overall entertainment business. As a business, you're competing against other types of entertainment. People have more options in terms of what to do with their leisure dollars. People who in the past maybe were gung ho or solidly spent their entertainment dollars on professional sports do not always do so anymore.

Many people don't think of professional sports as a business; they think of it more in terms of sport, but it certainly is a business – more so now than ever before. Payroll costs (player costs) are substantial, and I think more and more sports franchises are trying to operate as businesses rather than simply a sports company. You have to evaluate your market and your competition within your sport. You have budgets and marketing and sales and projections and all the same aspects and elements that a normal business has.

If you look at the major sports – football, baseball, basketball, and hockey – hockey is different in that a higher percentage of its revenue is based on ticket sales. We don't have the national TV contracts that the other sports have. I think that makes the NHL as a business more fragile, as it is still primarily ticket-driven.

A professional sports executive – general manager or coach – is scrutinized publicly every day by the media. During our season we are scrutinized, criticized, and analyzed on a daily basis by all types of media vehicles. I believe that is significantly different than being a CEO or a top executive at another type of business. There's the publicness of it, as well as the emotion of it. We always say that stockbrokers hear from their clients when stocks are down; we hear from our fans when our teams are down. In one sense, this should not affect the way you do your job at all; you still have to do what you and your people think is right. But you certainly have to consider how you present it. I do not take the view that the media is the enemy, but I also do not take the view that you have to do something because the media told you to do it. Certainly, because of the publicness of our business, you are always considering the timing and how something will be accepted by your fans and your market. Much of that is going to be influenced by the media.

The Team: The Chicago Blackhawks

As the general manager of the Blackhawks, I am in charge of the hockey operations – everything that goes on in the hockey area in terms of the two teams on the ice, the coaches, the two scouting departments that find our players, the ultimate expenditures in dollars, and trading of players. Ultimately, even if it is not my decision, I am responsible for the decisions that other people make. Several years ago the general manager was in charge of the business and the hockey, but now a general manager in the National Hockey League is usually in charge of the hockey operations, which usually represent at least 80 percent of the dollars and more than 80 percent of the workforce, the players, and the trainers.

I do not think any one team is unique in the way that they do business, although teams are operated in different ways. Some teams are looking to sign free agents and spend money to bring in players. Other franchises want to build through the draft and put more emphasis on the player development. Everywhere I have worked we have put emphasis on the draft. We do look at free agency, though. There are two schools: there's one school that signs free agents and there's another school that says not to sign free agents but draft players and bring your own players along. I am in between; I put great importance on the draft, but I also look at free agency as a way to build the team at the same time.

We're in a rebuilding process right now. We put great emphasis on the draft. We're in a situation in which many of our drafted players are getting close to making our team. Many players never play in the minor leagues in the NHL. The top players go directly from wherever they're playing – college or junior hockey or Europe – to the big team. If a team is down and out, there are two ways to rectify it. One is free agents, which is the quick fix and does not always work. The other is to be more patient, take some time, and do it through the draft. We have worked mostly through the draft, but we also look at free agents.

We have had 48 draft picks in the last four years. The normal number is 36. I think our Chicago fans are now following our prospects and where they're playing. I think all fans also like to see an instant change in their team through a trade or free agency. Player movement is very popular in our industry and generates a great deal of fan interest.

Prior to starting a negotiation, we do an analysis of where a player is in terms of dollars and what we think he should get paid. We attempt to make an offer relatively close to where we think we're going to end up; I do not lowball people, that's not part of my strategy. We do contract preparation, and if we think a player is worth X dollars, we offer close to X dollars.

Generally speaking, all success for a team is on the ice. This is a business in which winning – and doing well in the playoffs – is important. If you take a longer view of the Blackhawks, we have been very successful going as far back as the 1970s. In more recent years we've been less successful. That is probably one of the reasons I got hired. Right now we're on a bridge to becoming successful. I would say that this next year is important for the next 10 or 12 years of the Blackhawks. It is time for our young players that will carry the future to emerge.

Success for a General Manager

Ultimately, as a general manager, your success is determined by the quality of the team you put out on the ice. Generally speaking, it's the quality of the team and the amount of money you spend to do it. If you put a team on the ice with a payroll of $32 million and you are doing better than a team with a payroll of $60 million, then you are doing your job well, both competitively and businesswise.

Your job as a manager also includes managing part of the assets of the owners of the company. Managers are responsible for the assets of the company – for profits, losses, money spent. That is a part of any manager's job in any business.

As a general manager, you have to know the players, but you have to be able to pay the players what they're worth. If a player is a $1 million player and you're paying him $1.1 million, then that's better than paying him $2.5 million. That's part of managing the assets of the ownership. A player is assessed by what level he can play at. Is he a top defenseman, is he a top goalie, is he top-nine forward, is he a top-six forward? What level is he going to play at on your team? Many people may expect a young player drafted high to be a high-level player, and he might just turn out to be a mid-level player in the league. You need to make that assessment as you go along. Several things go into that assessment: talent, of course, but the other two areas are the quality of person he is (the character he brings, which is reflected in his desire to be successful) and his work ethic (whether or not he sees his own success determined by his individual performance or that of the team). There have been years in which there has been a pool of talented players that did not have the characteristics and values that would allow them to become successful team members.

I attend about 80 percent of all our games – about 170 games a year as a manager. You attend fewer as a manager than as a scout; a scout may see 250 games. The coach is at every game. The ownership is at home games.

I look at things in terms of vision. The coach has a vision of 30 days to a year, the manager has a vision of 3 to 5 years, the team president up to 10 years, and the owner 20 to 25 years. As a manager, you have to keep in mind that what you're doing now in this 4- or 5-year period does not end after the five years; it is not finite. It's tied into another period afterward. Everything is tied in to what we do now because if it does not work out, you put the franchise at some risk. You have to recognize that the time period of your vision is part of a continuum.

The Structure of the Organization

The structure of the management is such that there is an assistant general manager, then there is a director or manager of scouting, and he has a staff of about 10 to 15 people – it varies from team to team – of full- and part-time scouts. There is a new phenomenon of a pro-scouting department. There is the big team's coaching staff, training staff, and players. There is the farm team, and again there is the management, the coaching staff, the training staff, and the players. That is the hockey part of the organization. It varies a little bit from organization to organization, but we all have a manager, a scouting department, a team, a minor league team, and most of us have a pro-scouting department now.

The owner has a great deal of impact in his patience or his lack of it, his understanding or lack of it (with regard to what you're doing), and his resolve or lack of it. The owner is someone who is also very public in this business. He may have owned many businesses, but no one reads about him until he buys a basketball team or a football team. The ownership is extremely important in how successful an organization is.

The coaches and coaching staff are also important, of course. They are the ones who are in charge of the teams that play the games, which are our major product. The direction that the individual players and the players as a team get certainly comes from the coaches and the coaching staff. It is a very critical position. Whenever you hire a coach, you hope you're hiring a coach for the next 10 years and that things are going to work out. Hiring a coach is a little different process from obtaining players. There are veteran coaches who have been in the league for a while, and then there are emerging young coaches who are coaching in the farm leagues or who have been assistant coaches. Obviously the experienced coach is better known and has an advantage in getting a job. There is quite a bit of movement in the coaching area. I think in all sports – college, professional – because of the relationship between a group of players and a coach, and the job a coach has in dealing with the players on an everyday basis, quite often the coach is held more directly responsible for how the team is doing than are other people in the organization. He's in charge of the actual team on a day-to-day basis. He has that responsibility.

Scouting, in the hockey business, is our research and development. If the scouting system can consistently deliver better players, the team will have a better chance at being competitive. Scouting is important both at the amateur level, which we call the entry draft, and at the professional level, where we might sign players as free agents or trade for them.

Revenue and Profitability

Revenue comes mainly from ticket sales. There are also TV and radio contracts, advertising, and programs, but that's about it. Concessions vary from team to team. Generally a good part of concession revenue goes to the building. United Center is owned by the Bulls and the Blackhawks. It's a separate entity; it's totally separate from the two sports teams.

We all have our own practice facilities; no one practices on a daily basis in their regular game facility. This is true of every team. Occasionally a team can practice in its building, but teams have lease agreements with the buildings they play in, and that lease agreement can be a factor. Most leases in the NHL are long-term leases, but the general manager of the hockey team is not really involved in that.

Memorabilia sales are not substantial revenue generators. There are jerseys and that type of material, but that's not substantial. The most important thing is that you have to sell your seats. This applies more to hockey than to any other professional sport. We don't have the national television contracts that baseball, football, and basketball have. That would influence ticket prices.

Having a consistently winning team affects profits. We're in the process of rebuilding through the draft to ensure this for our team. I think you have to have a flow of a pipeline of players. You have to have young players who are going to be ready to come into your team and replace some of the older players and maintain a level of play that will keep your team competitive. Generally speaking, younger players will make less money than the older players.

I think everyone would like to have players who play their entire career with one team, but unfortunately it does not work that way. Players all get the right to unrestricted free agency, and they usually end up leaving to go elsewhere for more money. There is fan identity with the individual players, and it is important to have a core of players that remain with your team year after year. That core changes as some players get older and they leave and are replaced with younger players. The Blackhawks are quite loyal to their players; they would like their players to stay here as long as possible. As in any other profession, though, if someone offers you twice your salary, you'd probably leave.

In hockey, the business can be viewed as being on a pendulum. There was a time when it had swung in the direction of clubs and ownership; now it has swung in the direction of the players. We need a correction of that pendulum. Right now the pendulum has swung so that players are extremely well paid, and teams' profitability is at risk, or even worse than that. We need to get our costs in line with our revenues. We have a collective bargaining agreement with the players' association which dictates a good deal of that. The agreement is up this coming season. There will eventually be a new collective bargaining agreement. It's much like the airline industry; costs are greater than revenues. Player costs take 75 cents of each revenue dollar. A small minority of teams are profitable right now.

A strong fan base is probably the most important key to profitability. We're a ticket-driven sport, so the fan base is the most important thing. To develop our fan base, we do a lot more community activities now, and we use our Web site, which is relatively new. Chicago has had a long reputation of supporting amateur hockey, and the Blackhawks' owners, the Wertz family, are very influential in the expansion of amateur hockey in the state of Illinois and Greater Chicago; that is one way to try to expand the market. The Web site is a vehicle that speaks directly to the fans. As opposed to getting a less than balanced view in the newspaper media, it's a way to put out your view of what you are doing and what is happening. In all markets, very little is written about hockey in the off-season. The Web site allows you to continue your communication with your fans 12 months a year.

Having a star player can also be a factor. Winning, apart from just being a championship team, is vital. To build a winning team, you're looking for athletes who have values that are team-oriented. You are looking for people who are driven to be successful; they don't accept being average and push themselves to make themselves better year in and year out and not become complacent. In professional sports, people sometimes become complacent because they make a great deal of money. You are always looking to add role players. It is always easier to make changes with lower or mid-level role players than it is with top-level players. In a team chemistry, role players are important.

To successfully manage a workforce of athletes, I think you have to be direct and honest and listen to what they have to say. You need the ability to get along and to build up some relationships with trust. In our business, it is a player business because players make up the biggest portion of the team and the fans identify with the team and the players. Players need to know that the managers and coaches are putting the players and the team above everything. They're the product. I think that's very important. If the coach or the manager is more of an "I" driven person, once the players and the team read that, then the relationship begins to break down.

Changes in the Business

In the sports business, if you lose enthusiasm for the game, you're in trouble. I think that may be the key difference between the sports business and other businesses. If you're in another business and you are sick of selling something, you could go into another industry. Here, you have to maintain a level of enthusiasm for the game – and it is a game. At times it is a difficult career, but it beats having a regular job.

The business has changed a great deal in the last few years. As players' salaries have risen, the business has changed a lot in terms of making decisions based on players and factoring in the amount of money you have to pay them. The average salary has gone in the last 10 years from $750,000 to $1.8 million, so team payrolls have gone from $10–12 million to $25–70 million. The more dollars you're responsible for, the more costly mistakes are.

Future changes will be determined when there is a new collective bargaining agreement. That will determine the relationship between the clubs and the players. In professional sports, the collective bargaining agreement is extremely important to the profitability and the overall success of the sport because the player costs are so high. It's an agreement between the players, the players' union, and the league (the NHL, which is composed of 30 teams and surrounded by the commissioner and staff). It has a lot to do with the mechanisms used in dealing with the players as a group – their rights, the ownership's right in dealing with the players, the players' rights to various forms of free agency, and so on. The current collective bargaining agreement is about 350 pages long and pretty difficult to read. It's an extensive labor agreement between the players and the league. It addresses medical expenses, leaves of absence when players are hurt, moving expenses when players are traded – those kinds of things.

If I could change one thing it would be to bring players' salaries back to more reasonable levels. I think that high salaries have negatively affected the competitiveness of many individual players. The average salary of a hockey player is higher than that of a football player. We don't have those gargantuan $100 million contracts like basketball and baseball, but the average salary this year is $1.79 million. That's pretty good pay for an average.

Mike Smith began his career with the NY Rangers in 1976. He held coaching jobs in New York, Colorado and Winnipeg. In Winnipeg he moved into scouting and management. Smith has managed the Winnipeg Jets, the Toronto Maple Leafs, and the Chicago Blackhawks. He has authored 10 books, mostly on coaching, and Life After Hockey: When the Lights are Dimmed, a book about the transition of Pro players from the game to a normal life. He received the Co-Executive of the Year award in 1999 from The Hockey News, and the NHL Executive of the Year in 2002 from The Sporting News. Mike holds a PH.D. from Syracuse University in Political Science and Russian Studies.

A Winning Tradition

Joe Garagiola, Jr.

Senior Vice President and General Manager
Arizona Diamondbacks

Sports Business

The sports business, first of all, is a subset of the overall entertainment industry. We are in a business that, in large measure, depends on discretionary income. In difficult economic times, attending a sporting event is something that can easily be cut out of a family's budget. The sports franchise operator must constantly be examining the product to make the entire experience attractive. While there are many parallels between the sports business and other elements of the entertainment industry, our business is in a very important way unique, because the bottom line is so tied to results on the field. The element of randomness is so prevalent. In the operation of a professional sports team, management spends a great deal of time on analysis. By way of example, in baseball, we spend literally hundreds of hours in preparation for the amateur draft. Advance scouts prepare reports on the tendencies of opposing teams for the use of the manager and coaches. Other scouts write reports on players who might be considered in trades, or be signed as free agents. But no matter how much time is spent, or how thorough the analysis is, the element of randomness always seems to intrude. Someone is injured at an inopportune moment, a veteran player you are really counting on doesn't come through, or an untested rookie gets a chance and outperforms everyone's expectations. This element of unpredictability gives sports its unique appeal.

As do other industries, baseball invests heavily in what might be termed "research and development." We call our R&D department the minor leagues, or player development, where we spend as an industry tens of millions of dollars annually. On its face, our player development system does not appear to be very efficient in that, from a statistical standpoint, relatively few of the players who are drafted and signed achieve success in the major leagues. While this is a somewhat depressing fact (particularly to those responsible for the drafting and signing of these players), it is probably not terribly different from the experience of businesses in general, where you spend a lot of money pursuing new ideas that don't work out. It's always a sobering moment the day before the amateur draft when you look at the draft board, with literally hundreds and hundreds of names on it. You always look at those names and say, if you just knew which ones could play, those would be the ones we would pick, and we would leave the rest alone. This must be the same feeling that editors have at publishing houses as they read manuscript after manuscript and say, "If we just knew which one people wanted to read, we would publish that one and throw away the rest of them." Everyone spends an inordinate amount of time trying to eliminate as much uncertainty as possible. We study statistics, looking for reliable predictors. New statistics are developed regularly that are immediately seized upon as "the stat." Analysis has become more and more sophisticated, but the human element which underlies the sports business will always, to some degree, defy the most sophisticated analysis. First-round picks fail, while low-round picks become All-Stars. Fans, of course, really don't care about much of this. They want to see their team win. So, at all times, you have the competing considerations of running a business in a prudent fashion and satisfying the desire of your fans, your customers, by putting a winning product on the field. Michael Eisner probably said it best when he was asked why Disney was thinking about selling the Anaheim Angels. He said that if they ran the Angels in a way that made the Disney shareholders happy, the fans of Orange County probably wouldn't like it. If they ran the Angels in a way to make the fans happy, the shareholders of Disney probably wouldn't like it. That statement succinctly summarizes the dilemma often faced by the management of a professional team.

Role with Diamondbacks

I am the Senior Vice President and the General Manager of the Diamondbacks. I am in charge of baseball operations. I report to Rich

Dozer, who is the President, and Jerry Colangelo, who is the Managing General Partner. Ultimately, anything that happens in baseball operations, which encompasses the Major League team and all of our minor league teams, and that includes scouting as well, is my responsibility.

The brief history of the Arizona Diamondbacks has been very much an atypical one in terms of how expansion teams have historically developed, but it represents a very conscious effort to design and execute a specific business plan. Our first season was in 1998. We played with a roster that was by and large composed of players that we had selected in the expansion draft. The expansion draft process was not intended to allow us to assemble a competitive roster, and neither we nor the Tampa Bay Devil Rays did so. We supplemented our 1998 expansion draft roster with some significant acquisitions. We signed infielder Jay Bell and pitcher Andy Benes as free agents, and traded for infielder Matt Williams and outfielder Devon White. We also stunned the baseball world when we signed a college first baseman named Travis Lee for $10 million. Lee had been taken with the second pick in the 1996 amateur draft, but because of a technical violation of the rules, was declared a free agent, able to sign with any team. Lee had won the Golden Spikes Award in 1996, baseball's version of the Heisman Trophy. We viewed his signing as a real coup, and a real indication to our fans that we would be committed from the beginning to putting a winning product on the field. We also felt that Travis Lee had the potential to become a true "franchise player," someone fans would see as the first true Diamondback, in that he hadn't come from somewhere else. Our first year produced a record of 65 wins and 97 losses, which was more or less in line with what first-year teams had historically accomplished. However, following the 1998 season, we experienced a dramatic drop in our season ticket renewals. This was something that was very different than what other expansion teams had experienced. We had expected to replicate the experience of the Colorado Rockies, an expansion team that we felt we were very similar to. The Rockies had tremendous attendance in the first few years of their existence, when they were playing in Mile High Stadium. When they moved into Coors Field, they were able to sustain that attendance, even when their performance on the field was not as successful as they hoped for. We concluded that for whatever reason, we were not going to be the beneficiaries of a multi-year honeymoon period. Perhaps because our fans had been able to watch Major League baseball each spring in the Cactus League, it became apparent that our fans were not going to be happy (and, more importantly, supportive) for the first 3-5 years of our existence solely because Major League baseball had now come to Phoenix.

So at that point, we faced a choice. One approach was to continue on the traditional path of expansion teams, which is to not be very good in the early years, wait for your farm system to develop young players, and gradually get better and better. If you look at the Toronto Blue Jays, their first year was 1977. They went 10 seasons before they played .500. Then, in the 90s they won the World Series in back to back years. But they went the first 10 years of their existence losing more games than they won. The other approach had never really been tried before. That approach was to acquire a number of good veteran players, by trades or by signing free agents, and see how good a team could immediately be put on the field while waiting for young players to develop. In a bold move that shocked baseball as much as our signing of Travis Lee had, Jerry Colangelo opted for the second approach. Our idea was to bring in a group of players and commit to a four-year run with that group of players, figuring that by the end of the 2002 season, our player development system should have matured to the point that we could reasonably expect it to be producing Major League players.

This strategy was premised not on some vague notion that it would be more fun to win than to lose, but out of the pragmatic concern that we needed to protect our season ticket base. We needed to put a product on the field that would be attractive to advertisers and that would sustain television ratings and would generally be attractive to fans. So that's what we did. We signed free agents. We traded for players. The centerpiece of all that activity was the signing of Randy Johnson. Randy came to Phoenix not, as was widely speculated, because we were going to pay him a lot of money and because he lived here, but because we were going to pay him a lot of money and because he felt that this team had a chance to be competitive. Randy had a great line at his press conference. He was asked the question, "So Randy, didn't you pick the Diamondbacks because you live here?" about ten times. And after about the tenth time, with a note of some asperity in his voice, he said, "Look, don't you think that for the amount of money teams were going to pay me, I could have bought a house anywhere I wanted to play?" Of course, the answer was yes. He said, "I am here because I see what this team has done. They signed Greg Colbrunn. They signed Todd Stottlemyre. They signed Armando Reynoso. They traded for Luis Gonzalez. They signed Greg Swindell. This team has a good chance to be competitive over the seasons that I have committed to be here. That's why I am here."

Nonetheless, many people were skeptical that one of the best pitchers in baseball had signed a four-year contract with a team that had lost nearly 100 games in the previous season. However, Randy turned out to be correct. In 1999 we won 100 games. It was the biggest single season turnaround in the history of baseball. We went from 65 wins to 100 wins. We won the western division championship, making the Diamondbacks the fastest team to win a division. We lost in the first round of the playoffs to the Mets. It was a heartbreaking loss to the Mets because, trailing two games to one, we had come back in the fourth game to take the lead. The Division Series is best three out of five. We were thinking ok, now we are going to win this game, fly back to Phoenix, and have Randy Johnson going in the fifth game for us. The game ended on a walk off home run on a ball that Steve Finley, a Gold Glove centerfielder, made probably the worst leap at the center field fence he has ever made in his career. In one of those rare moments where the right player is at the right place at the right time, Finley jumped straight back into the fence. Even at that, the ball just ticked off of his glove, but our season was over.

Ironically, we all had the opportunity to relive that moment the following season when we played the Mets in a regular-season game. Another ball was hit to center field, but this time, Finley went back, jumped up, got his glove about four feet above the fence, and brought the ball back. Even though we lost in 1999, it gave us a great deal of confidence. Going through that experience really set us up for what we set out to accomplish in 2001. There was a sense in 1999 that it was great just to reach the playoffs. By 2001, we knew that getting to the playoffs and losing in the first round was not a very fulfilling feeling. I think we took the experience of 1999 and used that. It was essentially, with one major exception, the same group of players in 2001 as we had in 1999.

I think that where we are now is that we are very much following the plan that we laid out back in the off-season of 1998 and 1999. The only way to have consistent long-term success is to develop your own players. You then supplement those players with players that you can acquire through trades and free agency, but the backbone of your organization simply must be players who come up through your system. I don't think there is really another way, particularly given the economics of the game today, to sustain continued success. You cannot afford to go out year after year and sign the most talented free agents that are on the market. Very few teams can afford to do that. You have to develop your own players. There is a very important business element to this approach. When we were putting together the 1999 team, we structured the contracts of many of those players with a lot of money deferred to later years. That was a very conscious decision. When those deferred payments became due, the goal was to have a competitive team with a much lower payroll. But that can't happen if every year we had gone out and signed a whole new group of expensive free agent players. We knew we would be relying on young players who are at a stage in their careers when they are not making a lot of money because that is how the system is set up. During the first three years of a player's career, he doesn't make a lot of money, and then he becomes eligible to have his salary set by an independent arbitrator. That's the first time when a player's salary can really ramp up. A few years after that, and the player becomes eligible for free agency, and the salaries ramp up again. Our goal was to establish a system that in the future could accomplish two equally important objectives: be competitive and have a payroll that we can manage at the same time that we deal with the deferred payments that are then coming due.

Minor Leagues

Over time, we have traded a number of minor league players. Many of the trades that we made were criticized at the time. The criticism was that we traded too much and gave away our best prospects, the players who were going to be big stars. By and large, that has not happened. The reason that it hasn't happened is because we know our own players. That is just a function of your own people, your player development people in particular, having a good feel for their own players. The Atlanta Braves historically are maybe the best at that kind of evaluation. John Schuerholz, the Braves General Manager, doesn't get nearly enough credit for what he has done in Atlanta. John and his people know their players. When the Braves make a trade, they seldom trade a player who goes on to become a big star. You look at the players who they kept and the players who they traded, (and I set Kevin Millwood aside because there were economic circumstances there that dictated that) and with the trades that they have made not under duress, the player that the Braves keep usually turns out to be in the long run a lot better than the player that they trade.

That is not an accident; it is knowing your players. I tell our player development people all the time that if we don't know our players better than scouts from other organizations, then shame on us. These are our players. We live with them every day. Of course, you can never know with certainty, and this gets back to the randomness factor. The oldest line that you can attribute to scouts and scouting is that if a scout could look inside a player's head and his heart, he would never make a mistake. That is so true. I don't know how much of a carry over to other businesses and industries that concept has, but in the sports business, we are confronted with it on a daily basis. The player who lights up the radar gun, or who has the scouts shaking their heads when they time him to first base and who hits balls in batting practice out of sight, turns out to be a mediocre Major League player. The player who did none of those things turns out to be a key player on a championship team. Why? How? The answer is that we don't really know. But to the best of your ability, you have to know your own players so that you can then accurately assess what it is that you are giving up in a deal.

Sometimes you have to give up a player that you think is going to be a really good player in order to get a really good player back. I love the sports call-in shows, when the topic of making trades comes up. The trade proposals are generally some version of "let's give them three of our bad players and get one of their really good players." I always say, "Sounds great, I would love to make a deal like that. I just can't convince the other guy to do it because he wants to do the same thing." So you have to know your players as well as you can, and you have to try to know the player that you are getting. It falls all along a spectrum, from the trade that helps both clubs to the trade that you were declared the big winner in to the trade that you are declared the big loser in. Hopefully you make more of one or two than you do three.

Trading will also sometime involve trying to maximize what is perceived as an opportunity. Two of our major trades, Matt Mantei in 1999 and

Curt Schilling in 2000, involved our sending away several of our young players. The Schilling deal included Travis Lee, in whom we had invested $10 million. But in both instances, we felt we had a chance to advance to post-season play by making these deals. We made the post-season in 1999, fell short in 2000, but in 2001 won the World Series, with Schilling playing a pivotal role throughout the regular season and the playoffs.

It may seem like a simplification that is beyond the obvious, but at this level, our goal is to win. There is, of course, no more of a guarantee that a team will win in some future year with players who make their way up from the minor leagues, than that they will win now with players acquired in trades involving those same young players. And a team that is constantly trading its best young players will soon find itself in the worst of all situations: No players to trade, and no young players to look to for the future. But there are moments when a team simply has to go for it, and put its future at some degree of risk. When are those moments, and how do you recognize them? I wish they came with an identifying label, but unfortunately, they don't. Decisions to pull the trigger on big deals come only after a great deal of discussion. And if you don't have trust and confidence in the people involved in that decision-making process, then you have the wrong people.

Revenue

Ticket sales still, even in this era of multiple revenue streams, make up the bulk of a team's revenue. Teams have had to become very creative in terms of trying to develop additional revenue streams. I always laugh at people who say, "Oh, I go to the ballpark and every place I look there seems to be advertising, and there is advertising between innings, and every game has a sponsor, and then I watch the game on TV and there are all of these commercial breaks, the wind-up was presented by this person and the call to the bullpen is presented by that company." The complaint is that things are now more "cluttered" than they used to be. And that is exactly right. Players don't play for $30,000 a year anymore. Fans want to watch a competitive team on the field. Simply put, they want their team to win. Usually, if the team does that, fans will buy tickets.

They also want the team to keep the ticket prices down. That is certainly something we want to do, since we want fans to buy tickets to eighty-one games, more than twice the number for basketball or hockey. To keep prices down, we have to do a lot of other things. Those other things include naming rights. Some "purists" were aghast at the concept of commercializing the name of a ballpark or a building. That is an important revenue stream. Ballpark advertising is an important revenue stream. Apparel generates revenue. There was a time when fans could not buy the same jerseys, jackets and caps that teams wore on the field. Baseball felt that it was important to preserve the actual uniform solely for play on the field. Now, a team may have a batting practice top, several jerseys and three different caps. If they are attractive and, more importantly, people see players actually wearing them, they will want to buy them, and that is more revenue. I always kid our Vice President for Sales and Marketing that he's in production, and I'm in distribution. He is trying to generate revenue, and Baseball Operations is trying to spend it. His goal is to stay ahead of me. So everything of a commercial nature that you see in the ballpark is there to increase revenues so that we aren't constantly raising ticket prices. Given the numbers of games we play at home, our fans need to be able to come to games frequently. We can't price our tickets so that attending a game in person becomes an annual event. That might work for the NFL, but it certainly doesn't work for baseball.

But, having a successful team is no guarantee of fan support. The days of fans filling up parks with uncomfortable seats, obstructed views, and inadequate concession and restroom facilities are gone, and, to borrow a line from Bruce Springsteen, "they ain't comin' back." Why, for example, does the Bank One Ballpark have a retractable roof? The answer is not because we thought it would be nice to spend an additional $50 million to have it, but because Phoenix, Arizona is a community located in a geographic area where for part of the baseball season, the weather is beautiful, and for part of the baseball season, the weather is extremely harsh. People who live in Phoenix are not going to sit outside anywhere to do anything when it's over 100 degrees, and that includes watching a baseball game. A team can't survive on the hard-core fans that will come out under any circumstances. Montreal is proving that. You can go to an Expos game, and on a given night, there will be 5,000-10,000 people there. They will be as involved in the game and as attentive and as knowledgeable as fans anyplace, but there are only 10,000 of them. That is wonderful, but that is not enough. You have to reach the person who is a lot more on the margins, who likes baseball well enough, but who also likes being in a festive atmosphere, who likes to be comfortable, who likes to get something to eat and to drink and generally have a pleasant evening, and if the team wins, that is great. If the team loses, at least that fan goes home having had a pleasant experience. That is the goal. The goal is to have the fan walk out of the ballpark on a given night saying, in effect, I had a nice time, and I'll come back. Baseball is not a sport that can survive on the person who samples us once or twice a year.

Getting People into the Ballpark

One of the things that we thought would happen was that there would be a noticeable spike in our attendance on nights when Randy Johnson pitched. The reason we believed this was that a starting pitcher in baseball is unique because he only plays during specific games. If you want to see Luis Gonzalez, Mark Grace, or Steve Finley play, then you can pretty much come out any night. If you want to see the everyday players play, then you can come out every night, and there they are. Few relief pitchers generate that kind of interest, and there is no guarantee that on the night you come to the Dodger came, they will get into a save situation so you can see Eric Gagne. A starting pitcher, however, pitches Tuesday, and then he doesn't pitch Wednesday, Thursday, Friday, or Saturday, and he pitches Sunday. Then he doesn't pitch Monday, Tuesday, Wednesday, or Thursday, and then he pitches Friday. We began to see some increases on nights that RJ pitched in 2001 and 2002, but in the first couple of years, we didn't see it at all. It was surprising to us and frankly a little disappointing. Our attendance was very good after winning the World Series. We also experienced a huge jump in our merchandise sales. People really wanted merchandise with the World Champion logo on it, so our sales of merchandise went way up. The Anaheim Angels had a similar experience in 2003 in terms of their attendance. While they struggled on the field, they set an all-time attendance record.

Managing an Athletic Work Force

I am not the direct supervisor of the players. That is the manager and the coaches. It is a real challenge to manage an athletic work force because it is a collection of elite athletes, players who have been probably the best player on their team since Little League. Now they are in the major leagues, which represent the very tip of the iceberg. If you take the population of males in this country and asked what percentage of them at one time or another in their lives wanted to be baseball players, the percentage would probably be in the 90s. It might be 99 percent. All of these millions of people somewhere along the line think this, and then the selection process begins. It winnows and winnows and winnows until finally you are down to 30 teams of 25 players each. So out of this group of literally millions of people, there are at any one time less than a thousand players in the Majors. It is inevitable that this group would be comprised of some very strong egos. Casey Stengel, the manager of the great New York Yankee teams of the 1940's and '50's was once asked what was the secret of managing. Stengel's answer could apply to any workforce situation. He said that on any team, you have five players who really love you, five players who really hate you, and the rest of them who haven't made their minds up yet. The trick, he said, is to keep the five who hate you away from the ones who haven't made their minds up yet.

The most important element in successfully managing a team is communication. Everything else, and I mean everything else, pales in comparison. On any team, there are players at all points along the way in both the season they are involved in, as well as their careers. Effective communication starts with the manager. The manager is the one who makes out the line-up card. That is the single most powerful tool that management possesses in terms of the players. Fining players for misdeeds might have had some impact in the distant past, but fining someone who makes $5 million fifty dollars for being late to a team meeting probably isn't going to do much. Players want to play, and not playing is not good for the ego. Baseball is, I believe, the only sport which got the name of the person in charge exactly right. While there is a great deal of coaching which goes on, even at the Major League level, the manager must first and foremost "manage" his players. Manage them in the sense of figuring out who plays better after the figurative pat on the back, and who needs the figurative kick in the backside.

The manager needs to be constantly communicating with his players, and one size definitely does not fit all. The veteran who is not playing may need to face the harsh truth that he just isn't good enough to keep his job. The young player being sent back to the minor leagues needs to understand that he's just not quite ready yet, but is still in the plans. The player who is going on the disabled list needs to hear from the doctor that he really is going to get better. And what applies down in the clubhouse applies equally in the front office and the ranks of player development and scouting.

Baseball and sports in general thrive on rumors. Someone has always heard something. There is always some deal in the works. Someone is always about to get sent out or released. The manager needs coaches who have their ears to the ground. They need to be telling him what's going around in the clubhouse, and who needs to be talked to. The concept of management by walking around is very much the model for success, at least in our business. Most players don't do particularly well with being called into the manager's office where they sit on one side of the desk and the manager sits on the other. Maybe it gives them a bad flashback to junior high school. The manager has to be aware of this, and he has to pick his spots. A manager needs to be a presence in the clubhouse. An "open-door" policy doesn't do much good if nobody walks through the door.

The good manager is walking all over the field during batting practice. He is in the outfield just having a conversation with the pitchers. He is talking with guys around the batting cage. The important thing is that he is communicating. While some delegating of this is acceptable, for the most part players want to hear things from the manager. When it comes to matters such as releases, assignments to the minor leagues, or placements on the disabled list, they expect to hear these things from me, and they have a right to that expectation. Bad news is bad news, no matter how it's delivered. Not only isn't it possible to portray something such as telling a player he's being released in a positive light, it would be insulting to the player to try. However, by communicating honestly, even when it's not what they want to hear, you can create an atmosphere of mutual respect, and that gets around your clubhouse, and eventually in the industry. Most players can accept bad news, if they feel they have been dealt with fairly and honestly. Even at this level, it is amazing to me that with all of the monetary success and the acclaim that players get, they still need the communication and the reassurance. They want to be told that they are important to the team even if they are not playing every day. We haven't forgotten about you. It is an essential truth that even though they are making X millions of dollars, they still have the same set of feelings and emotions as anyone. They want to be congratulated when they have done good work. When they are not being used, they want to be given an explanation why.

Players

Jay Bell was the first player of stature that we signed. We signed him just before the expansion draft. About a month after the draft we traded for Matt Williams. In both cases, we felt that they were players who were very good players in terms of their skills on the field. In addition, they were people of good character. I don't think that a good player and a good person represent mutually exclusive topics. There are players who are both. Those are the players that we want to get because those are the people who, given the length of the baseball season, are going to really become part of the fabric of the community. We want people to feel good when these players have success and feel badly for them when they don't have success. The puzzling thing was that we were initially criticized for this approach. People would say, do you guys think you are putting together a Boy Scout troop, or are you trying to reinvent the game? What we were really saying was that character matters. That is still something that we think of when we are considering a player.

We try to do as much homework as we can and to talk to as many people as we can. We ask our scouts to tell us about the guy not just as a player on the field, but as a person, and we ask them if he is the kind of guy who will fit into our system. Is he our kind of player? Again, if you aren't prepared to trust the opinions of the people you are asking, then you have the wrong people working for you. By and large, I think we have been successful in identifying players like that. It has worked. Luis Gonzalez is a tremendous player who has become without a doubt the most popular professional athlete who has ever played in Phoenix, not just because he hit 57 home runs in one year, but because of who he is and how he interacts with fans. People are happy when he has success, and they feel badly for him when he doesn't have success. This has been the way that Jerry has run the Suns for 30 years, and the Suns have certainly been enormously successful both on the court and in terms of being a part of the community. It was only logical and natural that we would adopt the same view with the Diamondbacks.

But this by no means is to suggest that we strive to have a team made up of 25 versions of the same player. Our clubhouse at any one time runs the gamut, from those players who are content to sit in front of their locker and survey the passing scene, to those who are always at the ready with the appropriate comment. There are, however, common threads. Respect for the game, and respect for teammates are paramount. We are fortunate to have truly great players, whose work ethic suggests a rookie who is trying to make the team. In that regard, I am fond of saying that it's like high school. The freshmen watch the seniors and try to copy them. When a team is in transition, with a mix of rookies and veterans, the conduct of the "seniors" becomes even more important. As with any employee who has given valuable service over a number of years, veteran players are entitled to certain privileges that rookies have to earn. Again, this is where communication comes into play. It may seem obvious, but sometimes a young player needs to be reminded that he doesn't yet have ten years in the big leagues. What is ironic is that many times the big stars act like the extra men, and vice versa. I have told more than one player that "If you're going to act like a diva, then you better put up diva numbers."

Salary negotiation is a critical aspect of dealing with players. A team is inevitably made up of players at various stages of their career; young players whose salaries are controlled by the team; middle level players whose salary can be set by an outside arbitrator; and finally free agents who are able to talk to a number of teams and really engage in a competitive bidding process. Agents play a crucial role in the salary negotiation process. As with any group of people, agents run the gamut from the very capable to the not so very capable. A good agent does his homework before the negotiation starts, and has an idea of where his player fits into the overall salary structure. Threats, shouting and table-pounding are fairly useless theatrics, and the good agents know that. One of the inherent problems with the salary arbitration process is that the club must speak negatively about the player. It's a real skill to be able to present the club's case in a way that doesn't overly personalize things.

My former law partner, Mike Gallagher, presents our cases, and he does a great job with that aspect of it. Unfortunately, it's very difficult for anyone to sit through a long presentation of their shortcomings and not take it out of the hearing room with them. While the player is always present for an arbitration hearing, he usually is not during salary negotiations. This can become problematic, and more than once I have asked to have the player present, if not in person than over the phone. Back to my favorite topic—communication. There are points in a negotiation where the player needs to hear something directly from me, not filtered by his agent. Again, the good agents have no problem with this, and will often welcome it. As I was an agent for many years, I think I have a better feel for the player-agent relationship than most General Managers.

One of the things that we have always tried to do from the beginning, and I think that it has been a very good thing for us, is to create a very positive, comfortable atmosphere for the players. There are all kinds of ways to do this, from having a comfortable clubhouse, to having a really nice area where players' families can go during the game, to being very accommodating if a player's family needs help finding a local doctor. This is all to the end of having our players speak about playing for the Diamondbacks in positive terms. Players will not lie to other players. Players will tell each other the truth. If we are talking to a free agent, one of our players will, usually unsolicited, call that player and say, "Hey, you need to be here. This is a tremendous place to play. The organization is first class. They treat you with respect. If you need anything or if your family needs anything, they are there. We are a good team, and we are competitive. The owner and the management do what it takes to win. You need to be part of this." That is a great thing, and has been critical in many of our free agent signings. Otherwise you are just throwing dollars at somebody.

I like to think that, given that so many players know about Arizona and Phoenix from spring training, we have built on that in terms of creating a work environment that is very attractive and in so doing have made our players our best recruiters. I really believe that in any kind of a close call between us and another team, the lean will be in our direction. That is a great thing to know and to be able to take out into the market. It is something that we are very cognizant of, and something that we work very hard to maintain. It may seem odd to place that kind of emphasis on what is really "employee morale" when so many of these employees are millionaires, but, on some levels, the concerns are similar to those which arise in any workforce. We have one person in our organization who is the liaison to the players' wives. If they have any issues, whether it's parking at the ballpark or finding a pediatrician, they know that they can call her and get the answers. That is more important than it might seem, because if there is a problem, such as if two nights in a row somebody parked in the wrong spot, then on night number three, the player will be sent to the ballpark with instructions to straighten it out. So as the player is driving to the park, he is thinking about not forgetting to get the parking problem fixed, instead of how to get the Dodgers out that night.

In a business where the outcome is often balanced on a knife's edge, we try to eliminate anything that detracts from a player's focus and concentration. We have made a concentrated effort to make the families comfortable. For example, we have a very comfortable area where the families wait after the game so they are not just milling around out in the hall. A lot of places don't have this. Creating the work environment and acknowledging and accommodating the families are a big thing, and it has paid tangible dividends.

Building a Tradition

I think that building a tradition is a bit of a grandiose way to put what we are trying to do. Our mission statement says: "The Arizona Diamondbacks' mission is to establish a winning tradition that embodies the genuine spirit of baseball, an organization to which all Arizonans will point with pride, which conducts its business with integrity and community responsibility so that Arizona's children will grow up knowing the rich tradition that has made baseball America's national pastime." That is what we are trying to do. We are trying to become a part of the community and to have the people who are a part of the community tap into the tradition of this game. In the early years, when the Cubs would come to town, there would be thousands of people wearing their Cubs hats and Cubs shirts. People would ask me if that made me mad. I would say no, absolutely not. For one thing, I am happy that they are here. I'm glad they came. Secondly, one of the great strengths of baseball, maybe its greatest strength, is the loyalty that people have for teams. If somebody comes to the Bank One Ballpark wearing their Cubs hat, it is probably because their father or their grandfather told them stories about watching Ernie Banks play in Wrigley Field when he was a kid, and living and dying with the Cubs in 1969, and all of that. If it's the Mets cap, then maybe when they were kids, they saw Tom Seaver pitch. Then they grew up and moved to

Arizona, but they have always still loved the Mets. That is great. What we want to do, by who our players are and how we play and how we conduct ourselves, is to instill those same emotions in our fans so that 10 or 15 years from now people are bringing their kids to the ballpark and saying, boy, I remember that first year; they weren't very good, but there was the one game that Matt Williams hit this walk off home run. Like anything, eventually there will be 400,000 people who will swear they were in the park for game seven of the World Series, but that is part of the lore of baseball.

We have already accomplished many things in which we take a lot of pride. We engineered the biggest single season turnaround in the history of the game. We were the fastest team to win a Division Championship and the fastest team ever to win a World Series, in our fourth season. Those are the objective marks that we have hit. The real goal is to become a part of this community, as corny or clichéd as it sounds. That is what I think about a lot on a given night when I see people coming into the ballpark and when I see families coming in with little kids, I think that, this has a chance 30 years from now to be a scene that is repeated. Only then that little kid down there tonight will be bringing his family in to watch the Diamondbacks play. Baseball has always been a bridge between generations. There are no right or wrong answers in the baseball debates. Someone who saw Tom Seaver pitch can argue that Roger Clemens is great, but Seaver is better. They are both right. That is what this is ultimately all about.

Keys to Success

You have to, as best as you can, know your own players. You have to have a plan that you can't abandon at the first sign of trouble, but you cannot be inflexible because so many events that are beyond your control can impact you. You always have to stay on your toes, but you can't overreact to a bad game or a bad stretch of games. Roland Hemond, who has been in the game over 50 years, told me early on that you should never make a decision about a player on the night of a bad game. Never make a decision about pulling the trigger on a trade, releasing somebody, or sending somebody to the minor leagues right after a game is over, because you get so emotionally wrapped up in every game.

Where we sit upstairs is right next to where our organist sits. Often, he'll have people in there with him. If I happen to bump into those people before the game I'll always tell them, look, you may hear a lot of yelling and screaming and odd things coming from next door. You just have to ignore that. From 8:30 in the morning to 7:00 at night, all of us in there are actually pretty rational human beings who conduct ourselves all day in a fairly rational way. Once the game starts, we are, insofar as any ability to influence events goes, just like any other group of fans. It's very easy to get wrapped up in the events of a particular game and make decisions on the spot. That is almost a guarantee of a bad decision. You have to divorce your emotions from the decision-making process, and that is hard to do, because the game is played with a lot of emotion.

Down on field level, things happen at a fast pace and there are no do-overs. It is easy to let your frustrations overtake you, but you have to put all of those things back in the box when the game is over and take an objective view of the decisions that you are making. Objectivity is sometimes painful, particularly when it involves a player who has been instrumental in past successes. One of Branch Rickey's maxims was that it's always better to trade a player a year too early, rather than a year too late. Recently, Oracle founder Larry Ellison used a sports analogy when describing his management style. He said, "I try to put the best team on the field, and that means as we grow and change-as the industry changes-sometimes we have to change players." All players understand that careers end; it's just that few of them ever think their career will end.

Nothing is more valuable than accurate information, and nothing is worse than taking action based upon information that later proves to be inaccurate. It's literally impossible for any one person to have first-hand knowledge of what is going on with a major league roster, six minor league teams, and an academy in a foreign country. The quality of the decisions that are made is in direct proportion to the quality of the information the decision is based upon. If a person relied upon for substantive information is unable to provide accurate information on a timely basis, that is a weak link that will surely break at the most inopportune moment. In the end, trust your information, trust your people, trust your instincts, and communicate, communicate, communicate.

The best testimony to the work of Joe Garagiola and his baseball operations department was the success of last year's club. Challenged by wearing a target as the defending World Series champs, the now three-time Western Division title holders had to rely on the depth of a bench and farm system to survive the rigors of a season that was challenged with injuries at several key positions. No general manager in expansion history with healthy players has achieved the success of Garagiola, with three division titles in five years, much less after losing the likes of Matt Williams, Jay Bell, Danny Bautista and Craig Counsell for extended periods due to injuries.

Joe Garagiola had served 25 years earlier as the general counsel and assistant to the president of the New York Yankees, earning a ring while employed in the Bronx. Taking advantage of the resources provided by ownership, Joe was the foreman of a construction team that assembled the fastest World Series winner in expansion baseball history. He fine tuned a club that had finished 12 games out of the hunt in 2000 after winning 100 games the year before. Included were the signings of Mark Grace and Reggie Sanders, both of whom provided outstanding numbers, while the quiet off-season discovery of Miguel Batista turned into one of the top bargains in the game.

Garagiola joined the Diamondbacks in March, 1995, when the franchise was awarded to the region, but it was his work on the Arizona Baseball Commission that served as a driving force in procuring major league baseball for the Valley. He served as vice-chairman of the Governor's Cactus League Task Force, and was a member of the Mayor's Professional Baseball Committee. From there he branched out to the Maricopa County Sports Authority, serving as chairman. Garagiola was also chairman of the Arizona Baseball Commission, the group best known for completing the task of convincing existing major league clubs that Phoenix and the region were ready to possess their own club. Garagiola made his move to the Valley in 1982, applying his law practice to the firm of Gallagher and Kennedy. His concentration was on sports law, and he was the chairman of the Phoenix Metropolitan Sports Foundation from 1985-87.

Garagiola was the 1998 recipient of the prestigious Institute of Human Relations Award from the American Jewish Committee. He is also a life member of the Thunderbirds, the group that procures and distributes charitable money through the highly successful Phoenix Open. Garagiola graduated from the University of Notre Dame in South Bend, IN, earning a B.A. cum laude in 1972. He earned his law degree from Georgetown University Law Center (J.D., 1975), and is admitted to practice law in Arizona, California and New York.

CEO Best Practices

Management & Leadership Strategies from 200+ C-Level Executives

This insider look at succeeding as a top executive is written by C-Level professionals (CEOs, CFOs, CTOs, CMOs) from the world's leading companies. Each executive shares their knowledge on how to get an edge in business, from leading a company to making money in a down economy to increasing your efficiencies in all areas of your business (marketing, financial, technology, hr, and more). Also covered are over 250 specific, proven innovative strategies and methodologies practiced by leading executives and CEOs that have helped them gain an edge. This report is designed to give you insight into the leading executives of the world, and assist you in developing additional ideas in all areas of your business that can help you be even more successful as a top executive.

WRITTEN BY C-LEVEL EXECUTIVES FROM COMPANIES AT: Advanced Fibre Communications, American Express, American Standard Companies, AmeriVest Properties, AT Kearney, AT&T Wireless, Bank of America, Barclays, BDO Seidman, BearingPoint (Formerly KPMG Consulting), BEA Systems, Best Buy, BMC Software, Boeing, Booz-Allen Hamilton, Corning, Countrywide, Credit Suisse First Boston, Deutsche Bank, Drake Beam Morin, Duke Energy, Ernst & Young, FedEx, First Consulting Group, Ford Motor Co., Frost & Sullivan, General Electric, IBM, Interpublic Group, KPMG, LandAmerica, Mack-Cali Realty Corporation, Merrill Lynch, Micron Technology, Milliman & Robertson, Novell, Office Depot, On Semiconductor, Oxford Health, PeopleSoft, Perot Systems, Prudential, Salomon Smith Barney, Staples, Tellabs, The Coca-Cola Company, Unilever, Verizon, VoiceStream Wireless, Webster Financial Corporation, Weil, Gotshal & Manges, Yahoo!

$219.95

Call 1-866-Aspatore (277-2867) to Order Today!

Management Best Sellers

Other Best Sellers

- Ninety-Six and Too Busy to Die - Life Beyond the Age of Dying - $24.95

- Technology Blueprints - Strategies for Optimizing and Aligning Technology Strategy & Business - $69.95

- The CEO's Guide to Information Availability - Why Keeping People & Information Connected is Every Leader's New Priority - $27.95

- Being There Without Going There - Managing Teams Across Time Zones, Locations and Corporate Boundaries - $24.95

- Profitable Customer Relationships - CEOs from Leading Software Companies on using Technology to Maxmize Acquisition, Retention & Loyalty - $27.95

- The Entrepreneurial Problem Solver - Leading CEOs on How to Think Like an Entrepreneur and Solve Any Problem for Your Team/Company - $27.95

- The Philanthropic Executive - Establishing a Charitable Plan for Individuals & Businesses - $27.95

- The Golf Course Locator for Business Professionals - Organized by Closest to Largest 500 Companies, Cities & Airports - $12.95

- Living Longer Working Stronger - 7 Steps to Capitalizing on Better Health - $14.95

- Business Travel Bible - Must Have Phone Numbers, Business Resources, Maps & Emergency Info - $19.95

- ExecRecs - Executive Recommendations for the Best Business Products & Services Professionals Use to Excel - $14.95

Call 1-866-Aspatore (277-2867) to Order